Decolonising the Mind

Gerald Moore in *Le Monde Diplomatique*
   ... the poet or storyteller, he argues, cannot perform his
   function within his own society unless he shares and enriches
   its tongue. The Kenyan government only moved decisively
   against him when he began to do precisely that, first
   imprisoning him, then driving him into exile. Shifting the
   burden of racism and post-imperial prejudice from literature
   is, however, a global task, and one which Ngugi is now
   obliged to pursue from [New York] and in English.
Anver Versi in *New African*
   For a long time, Ngugi's was a lone voice howling against the
   wind. Now people like Edward Said have joined in the war
   against cultural imperialism. Let battle commence.

Decolonising the Mind

Joan Riley on the *BBC World Service*
Decolonising the Mind is powerfully written and full of the
clarity and honesty we have come to expect from the man
who is probably the most important figure in contemporary
African literature.

Carl Wood in *The Christian Science Monitor*
Cut the Kenyan novelist Ngugi wa Thiong'o, and he bleeds
politics. He is passionately committed to the egalitarian
ideals of the 1950s Kenyan revolution against Great Britain –
a dedication well illustrated in this book of essays on cultural
politics. Ngugi's revolutionary fervor has not diluted his
literary achievement . . . The main target of his political ire,
here as always, is corruption in Africa among Western-
influenced rulers and business leaders.

Anne Walmsley in *The Guardian*
. . . many of the ideas are familiar from Ngugi's earlier critical
books, and earlier lectures, elsewhere. But the material here
has a new context, and the ideas a new focus . . .

Ned Thomas in *Planet – The Welsh Internationalist*
. . . one of the most important statements to come from
Black Africa . . .

Adewale Maja-Pearce in *The New Statesman*
In retrospect that literature characterised by Ngugi as 'Afro-
European' – the literature written by Africans in the
European languages – will come to be seen as part and parcel
of the uneasy period between colonialism and full
independence, a period equally reflected in the continent's
political instability as it attempts to find its feet. Ngugi's
importance – and that of this book – lies in the courage with
which he has confronted this most urgent of issues.

Ngũgĩ
wa Thiong'o

Decolonising the Mind

The Politics
of Language
in African Literature

James Currey
OXFORD

EAEP
NAIROBI

Heinemann
PORTSMOUTH (NH)

Dedication

This book is gratefully
dedicated to all those who
write in African languages,
and to all those who over
the years have maintained
the dignity of the literature,
culture, philosophy, and
other treasures carried by
African languages.

James Currey Ltd
73 Botley Road
Oxford OX2 0BS, England

East African Educational Publishers
PO Box 45314
Nairobi, Kenya

Heinemann
A division of Reed Publishing (USA) Inc.
361 Hanover Street
Portsmouth, New Hampshire 03801-3912
Offices and agents throughout the world

© Ngugi wa Thiong'o
1981, 1982, 1984 and 1986

First published 1986
Reprinted 1988, 1989, 1991,
1992, 1994 (twice) 1997

10 11 12 01

British Library Cataloguing in Publication Data
Ngũgĩ wa Thiong'o
   Decolonising the mind: the politics of
   language in African literature.
   1. African language—20th century—
   History and criticism
   I. Title
   809′.896   PL8010
ISBN 0-85255-501-6

Library of Congress Cataloguing in Publication Data
Ngũgĩ wa Thiong'o, 1938—
   Decolonising the mind.
   Includes bibliographical references
   and index.
   1. African literature—History and
   criticism.
   2. Africa—Languages—Political
   aspects. I. Title.
   PL8010.N48   1986   809′.889′6
   86-4683
ISBN 0-435-08016-4

Typeset by Pen to Print, Colne
Printed in Great Britain

Contents

Acknowledgements

'The Language of African Literature' has a long history. Part of it was originally given as a paper at a conference organised by The Writers Association of Kenya in December 1981 on the theme 'Writing for our Children'. A slightly altered version of the original paper was also given at a conference on Language and African Literature at the University of Calabar, Nigeria in 1982. The same version – again slightly altered – was tabled at the Zimbabwe International Book Fair in 1983 and subsequently published in an African Writers Association (AWA) newsletter in the same year. The present is an expanded version and goes very much beyond the scope of the one preceding it. An abridged version of this paper was first read at a university seminar at the Bayreuth University in July 1984. The same, only slightly' changed to suit the occasion, was read as the opening speech at the Conference on New Writing from Africa, at the Commonwealth Institute in London in December 1984. The paper, slightly abridged, was first published in *New Left Review* no. 150 in 1985.

'The Language of African Theatre' was also read at the University of Zimbabwe in August 1984 under the auspices of the Literature Department and the Zimbabwe Foundation for Education with Production.

'The Language of African Fiction' has also been read in Harare, Zimbabwe under the auspices of the Institute of Development Studies in August 1984 and at the Institute of Commonwealth Studies, University of London, in February 1985.

Preface

I was glad to be asked to give the 1984 Robb lectures in honour of Sir Douglas Robb, former Chancellor of Auckland University and one of New Zealand's most distinguished surgeons. Universities today, particularly in Africa, have become the modern patrons for the artist. Most African writers are products of universities: indeed a good number of them still combine academic posts and writing. Also, a writer and a surgeon have something in common – a passion for truth. Prescription of the correct cure is dependent on a rigorous analysis of the reality. Writers are surgeons of the heart and souls of a community. And finally the lectures would never have been written, at least not in the year 1984, without the invitation from Auckland University.

I want to thank the Chancellor, Dr Lindo Ferguson, the Vice-Chancellor, Dr Colin Maiden, the Registrar, Mr Warwick Nicholl and their staff for both the invitation and the warm reception. Professor Michael Neil and Mr Sebastion Black were meticulous and helpful in all the arrangements. They, together with Professor Terry Sturm and the staff of the English Department, made me feel at home. Thanks also to Wanjikū Kīariī and Martyn Sanderson for their friendship and constant attention during the visit and for readily participating in the lectures as actors with only short notice; to Professor Albert Wendt, the Samoan novelist, and his wife Jenny, who laid on a big reception for us at their home at the University of South Pacific, Fiji, and took time to drive us around Suva; to Pat Hohepa who arranged a very moving Maori welcome; and to all the Maori people inside and outside the University who welcomed us in their houses or places of work. *A sante sana!*

I felt particularly touched by the welcome I received from the Maori people and it will long live in my memory. There is a lot to learn from the culture of Maori people, a culture which has such vitality, strength and beauty: the vitality, strength and beauty of resistance. I was happy therefore that my lectures on 'The Politics of Language in African

Literature' coincided with Maori language week. Long live the language and the struggling culture of the Maori people!

Apart from the stimulus of the New Zealand invitation, the lectures owed a lot to the time I spent at the Bayreuth University in West Germany as a Guest Professor attached to the Department of English and Comparative Literature from 15 May to 15 July 1984. I want to thank Professor H. Ruppert, co-ordinator of the special research project on identity in Africa, and the German Research Council for the invitation; and Professor Richard Taylor and the entire staff of the English department for their warm reception. I would like to single out Dr Reinhard Sander (who arranged the visit), Dr Rhonda Cobham, Dr Eakhard Breitinger, Dr Jurgen Martini and Margit Wermter, for making their time available and for providing me with a cosy and stimulating intellectual atmosphere for work. To Dr Bachir Diagne from Senegal, with whom I shared the house at St Johannes village, I feel a special indebtedness for all the sessions on mathematical logic, Louis Althusier, Michael Pêcheux, Pierre Macherey, Ferdinand de Saussure, Leopold Sédar Senghor, Wolof, African philosophy and much more. He also did translations of some passages from French into English.

The fact that these lectures were ready in time for delivery owed a lot to Eva Lannö. Although the first lecture was written and the general framework of the rest worked out in Bayreuth, the actual composition and writing of the other three and the typing of all four was done in New Zealand. Eva typed them, the last two as I was writing them, amidst working out the travel plans and appointments and rushing to the libraries and bookshops for urgently needed references.

And finally these lectures would not have been possible without the inspiring patriotic friendship of all my Kenyan compatriots abroad, particularly those in Britain, Denmark, Sweden and Zimbabwe; and to all the friends of Kenyan people's struggles for democratic and human rights. I don't mention their names here for reasons that lie outside this book. But the strength to write the lectures and other books I have written since 1982 under the harsh conditions of my present existence has come from them.

Over the years I have come to realise more and more that work, any work, even literary creative work, is not the result of an individual genius but the result of a collective effort. There are so many inputs in the actual formation of an image, an idea, a line of argument and even sometimes the formal arrangement. The very words we use are a product of a collective history. So, too, is the present work.

I owe a lot to the people who have contributed to the great debate on the language of African literature, in particular to the late David Diop of Senegal, and to Obi Wali of Nigeria who made the historic intervention in 1964. There are many others. African linguists for instance have been more progressive in their outlook on the language issue than their counterparts in creative literature. For instance, a lot of good work on Kenyan and African languages has been done at the Department of Linguistics and African languages at the University of Nairobi. Professor Abdulaziz and Dr Karega Mũtahi have done pioneering work in many areas of Kenyan languages. They both acknowledge the reality of there being three languages for each child in Kenya, a reality which many patriotic and democratic Kenyans would now argue should be translated into social and official policy. Kiswahili would be the all-Kenya national and official language; the other nationality languages would have their rightful places in the schools; and English would remain Kenya people's first language of international communication. But in these lectures I am not dealing so much with the language policies as with the language practice of African writers. I should here point out and reiterate that there are many writers all over Africa who over the years, over the centuries, have written and continue to write in African languages.

My thinking has been decisively shaped and changed more than I can ever express on paper by the collective work and debates of the staff and students of the Literature Department, University of Nairobi, particularly in the period from 1971 to 1977. I have always remembered with fondness all the staff and the students and the secretaries and all the other workers with whom I had the privilege to interact during those momentous years. Professor Mĩcere Mũgo had a capacity of firing my imagination in different directions and I looked forward, particularly in the years from 1974 to 1976, to our almost daily morning sessions of discussions and review of events in the corridors of the Literature Department, sessions which resulted in the joint authorship of *The Trial of Dedan Kĩmathi*, itself an act of literary and political intervention.

The 1974 Nairobi conference on the teaching of African literature in schools was an important landmark in my growth. I owe a lot to all the teachers and all the participants for I gained insights from the often heated proceedings. The conference itself owed much to the indefatigable efforts of S. Akivaga and Eddah Gachukia who ably and admirably held it together. To Wasambo Were, the first Kenyan inspector of drama and literature in the Ministry of Education, and to all the teachers and the staff of literature departments at Nairobi and at Kenyatta University College who have continued the debate on African literature in schools, I offer these essays as what would have been my contribution had I been on the scene.

If the Literature Department at Nairobi was influential in my thinking on language and literature, it was Kamĩrĩĩthũ that was decisive in my actual break with my past praxis, in the area of fiction and theatre. I am grateful to all the women and men of Kamĩrĩĩthũ with whom I worked at Kamĩrĩĩthũ Community Education and Cultural Centre, and in particular to Ngũgĩ wa Mĩriĩ, S. Somji, Kĩmani Gecau and Kabiru Kĩnyanjui.

Inevitably, essays of this nature may carry a holier-than-thou attitude or tone. I would like to make it clear that I am writing as much about myself as about anybody else. The present predicaments of Africa are often not a matter of personal choice: they arise from an historical situation. Their solutions are not so much a matter of personal decision as that of a fundamental social transformation of the structures of our societies starting with a real break with imperialism and its internal ruling allies. Imperialism and its comprador alliances in Africa can never never develop the continent.

If in these essays I criticise the Afro-European (or Euroafrican) choice of our linguistic praxis, it is not to take away from the talent and the genius of those who have written in English, French or Portuguese. On the contrary I am lamenting a neo-colonial situation which has meant the European bourgeoisie once again stealing our talents and geniuses as they have stolen our economies. In the eighteenth and nineteenth centuries Europe stole art treasures from Africa to decorate their houses and museums; in the twentieth century Europe is stealing the treasures of the mind to enrich their languages and cultures. Africa needs back its economy, its politics, its culture, its languages and all its patriotic writers.

To end with Shabaan Robert: *Titi la mama litamu lingawa la mbwa, lingine halishi tamu . . . Watu wasio na lugha ya asili, kadiri walivyo wastaarabu, cheo chao ni cha pili dunia – dunia la cheo.*

A Statement

In 1977 I published *Petals of Blood* and said farewell to the English language as a vehicle of my writing of plays, novels and short stories. All my subsequent creative writing has been written directly in Gĩkũyũ language: my novels *Caitaani Mũtharabainĩ* and *Matigari Ma Njirũũngi*, my plays *Ngaahika Ndeenda* (written with Ngũgĩ wa Mĩriĩ) and *Maitũ Njugĩra*, and my childrens' books, *Njamba Nene na Mbaathi ĩ Mathagu*, *Bathitoora ya Njamba Nene* and *Njamba Nene na Cibũ Kĩng'ang'i*.

However, I continued writing explanatory prose in English. Thus *Detained: A Writer's Prison Diary*, *Writers in Politics* and *Barrel of a Pen* were all written in English.

This book, *Decolonising the Mind*, is my farewell to English as a vehicle for any of my writings. From now on it is Gĩkũyũ and Kiswahili all the way.

However, I hope that through the age old medium of translation I shall be able to continue dialogue with all.

Introduction

This book is a summary of some of the issues in which I have been passionately involved for the last twenty years of my practice in fiction, theatre, criticism and in teaching literature. For those who have read my books *Homecoming*, *Writers in Politics*, *Barrel of a Pen* and even *Detained: A Writer's Prison Diary* there may be a feeling of *déjà vu*. Such a reaction will not be far from the truth. But the lectures on which this book is based have given me the chance to pull together in a connected and coherent form the main issues on the language question in literature which I have touched on here and there in my previous works and interviews. I hope though that the work has gained from the insights I have received from the reactions – friendly and hostile – of other people to the issues over the same years. This book is part of a continuing debate all over the continent about the destiny of Africa.

The study of the African realities has for too long been seen in terms of tribes. Whatever happens in Kenya, Uganda, Malawi is because of *Tribe A* versus *Tribe B*. Whatever erupts in Zaire, Nigeria, Liberia, Zambia is because of the traditional enmity between *Tribe D* and *Tribe C*. A variation of the same stock interpretation is *Moslem* versus *Christian* or *Catholic* versus *Protestant* where a people does not easily fall into 'tribes'. Even literature is sometimes evaluated in terms of the 'tribal' origins of the authors or the 'tribal' origins and composition of the characters in a given novel or play. This misleading stock interpretation of the African realities has been popularised by the western media which likes to deflect people from seeing that imperialism is still the root cause of many problems in Africa. Unfortunately some African intellectuals have fallen victims – a few incurably so – to that scheme and they are unable to see the divide-and-rule colonial origins of explaining any differences of intellectual outlook or any political clashes in terms of the ethnic origins of the actors. No man or woman can choose their biological nationality. The conflicts between peoples cannot be explained in terms of that which is fixed (the invariables). Otherwise the problems between any two peoples

1

would always be the same at all times and places; and further, there would never be any solution to social conflicts except through a change in that which is permanently fixed, for example through genetic or biological transformation of the actors.

My approach will be different. I shall look at the African realities as they are affected by the great struggle between the two mutually opposed forces in Africa today: an imperialist tradition on one hand, and a resistance tradition on the other. The imperialist tradition in Africa is today maintained by the international bourgeoisie using the multinational and of course the flag-waving native ruling classes. The economic and political dependance of this African neo-colonial bourgeoisie is reflected in its culture of apemanship and parrotry enforced on a restive population through police boots, barbed wire, a gowned clergy and judiciary; their ideas are spread by a corpus of state intellectuals, the academic and journalistic laureates of the neo-colonial establishment. The resistance tradition is being carried out by the working people (the peasantry and the proletariat) aided by patriotic students, intellectuals (academic and non-academic), soldiers and other progressive elements of the petty middle class. This resistance is reflected in their patriotic defence of the peasant/worker roots of national cultures, their defence of the democratic struggle in all the nationalities inhabiting the same territory. Any blow against imperialism, no matter the ethnic and regional origins of the blow, is a victory for all anti-imperialistic elements in all the nationalities. The sum total of all these blows no matter what their weight, size, scale, location in time and space makes the national heritage.

For these patriotic defenders of the fighting cultures of African people, imperialism is not a slogan. It is real, it is palpable in content and form and in its methods and effects. Imperialism is the rule of consolidated finance capital and since 1884 this monopolistic parasitic capital has affected and continues to affect the lives even of the peasants in the remotest corners of our countries. If you are in doubt, just count how many African countries have now been mortgaged to IMF – the new International Ministry of Finance as Julius Nyerere once called it. Who pays for the mortgage? Every single producer of real wealth (use-value) in the country so mortgaged, which means every single worker and peasant. Imperialism is total: it has economic, political, military, cultural and psychological consequences for the people of the world today. It could even lead to holocaust.

The freedom for western finance capital and for the vast trans-national monopolies under its umbrella to continue stealing from the countries and people of Latin America, Africa, Asia and Polynesia is today protected by conventional and nuclear weapons. Imperialism, led by the USA, presents the struggling peoples of the earth and all those calling for peace, democracy and socialism with the ultimatum: accept theft or death.

The oppressed and the exploited of the earth maintain their defiance: liberty from theft. But the biggest weapon wielded and actually daily unleashed by imperialism against that collective defiance is the cultural bomb. The effect of a cultural bomb is to annihilate a people's belief in their names, in their languages, in their environment, in their heritage of struggle, in their unity, in their capacities and ultimately in themselves. It makes them see their past as one wasteland of non-achievement and it makes them want to distance themselves from that wasteland. It makes them want to identify with that which is furthest removed from themselves; for instance, with other peoples' languages rather than their own. It makes them identify with that which is decadent and reactionary, all those forces which would stop their own springs of life. It even plants serious doubts about the moral rightness of struggle. Possibilities of triumph or victory are seen as remote, ridiculous dreams. The intended results are despair, despondency and a collective death-wish. Amidst this wasteland which it has created, imperialism presents itself as the cure and demands that the dependant sing hymns of praise with the constant refrain: 'Theft is holy'. Indeed, this refrain sums up the new creed of the neo-colonial bourgeoisie in many 'independent' African states.

The classes fighting against imperialism even in its neo-colonial stage and form, have to confront this threat with the higher and more creative culture of resolute struggle. These classes have to wield even more firmly the weapons of the struggle contained in their cultures. They have to speak the united language of struggle contained in each of their languages. They must discover their various tongues to sing the song: 'A people united can never be defeated'.

The theme of this book is simple. It is taken from a poem by the Guyanese poet Martin Carter in which he sees ordinary men and women hungering and living in rooms without lights; all those men and women in South Africa, Namibia, Kenya, Zaire, Ivory Coast, El Salvador, Chile, Phillipines, South Korea, Indonesia, Grenada, Fanon's 'Wretched of the Earth', who have declared loud and clear that they do not sleep to dream, 'but dream to change the world'.

I hope that some of the issues in this book will find echoes in your hearts.

1

The Language
of African Literature

I

The language of African literature cannot be discussed meaningfully outside the context of those social forces which have made it both an issue demanding our attention and a problem calling for a resolution.

On the one hand is imperialism in its colonial and neo-colonial phases continuously press-ganging the African hand to the plough to turn the soil over, and putting blinkers on him to make him view the path ahead only as determined for him by the master armed with the bible and the sword. In other words, imperialism continues to control the economy, politics, and cultures of Africa. But on the other, and pitted against it, are the ceaseless struggles of African people to liberate their economy, politics and culture from that Euro-American-based stranglehold to usher a new era of true communal self-regulation and self-determination. It is an ever-continuing struggle to seize back their creative initiative in history through a real control of all the means of communal self-definition in time and space. The choice of language and the use to which language is put is central to a people's definition of themselves in relation to their natural and social environment, indeed in relation to the entire universe. Hence language has always been at the heart of the two contending social forces in the Africa of the twentieth century.

The contention started a hundred years ago when in 1884 the capitalist powers of Europe sat in Berlin and carved an entire continent with a multiplicity of peoples, cultures, and languages into different colonies. It seems it is the fate of Africa to have her destiny always decided around conference tables in the metropolises of the western world: her submergence from self-governing communities into colonies was decided in Berlin; her more recent transition into neo-colonies along the same boundaries was negotiated around the same tables in London, Paris, Brussels and Lisbon. The Berlin-drawn division under which Africa is still living was obviously economic and political, despite the claims of bible-wielding diplomats, but it was also cultural. Berlin in 1884 saw the division of Africa into the different languages of the European powers. African countries, as colonies and even today as neo-colonies, came to be defined and to define themselves in terms of the languages of Europe: English-speaking, French-speaking or Portuguese-speaking African countries.[1]

Unfortunately writers who should have been mapping paths out of that linguistic encirclement of their continent also came to be defined and to define themselves in terms of the languages of imperialist imposition. Even at their most radical and pro-African position in their sentiments and articulation of problems they still took it as axiomatic that the renaissance of African cultures lay in the languages of Europe. I should know!

II

In 1962 I was invited to that historic meeting of African writers at Makerere University College, Kampala, Uganda. The list of participants contained most of the names which have now become the subject of scholarly dissertations in universities all over the world. The title? 'A Conference of *African Writers of English Expression*'.[2]

I was then a student of *English* at Makerere, an overseas college of the University of London. The main attraction for me was the certain possibility of meeting Chinua Achebe. I had with me a rough typescript of a novel in progress, *Weep Not, Child*, and I wanted him to read it. In the previous year, 1961, I had completed *The River Between*, my first-ever attempt at a novel, and entered it for a writing competition organised by the East African Literature Bureau. I was keeping in step with the tradition of Peter Abrahams with his output of novels and autobiographies from *Path of Thunder* to *Tell Freedom* and followed by Chinua Achebe with his publication of *Things Fall Apart* in 1959. Or there were their counterparts in French colonies, the generation of Sédar Senghor and David Diop included in the 1947/48 Paris edition of *Anthologie de la nouvelle poésie nègre et malgache de langue française*. They all wrote in European languages as was the case with all the participants in that momentous encounter on Makerere hill in Kampala in 1962.

The title, 'A Conference of African Writers of English Expression', automatically excluded those who wrote in African languages. Now on looking back from the self-questioning heights of 1986, I can see this contained absurd anomalies. I, a student, could qualify for the meeting on the basis of only two published short stories, 'The Fig Tree (Mūgumo)' in a student journal, *Penpoint*, and 'The Return' in a new journal, *Transition*. But neither Shabaan Robert, then the greatest living East African poet with several works of poetry and prose to his credit in Kiswahili, nor Chief Fagunwa, the great Nigerian writer with several published titles in Yoruba, could possibly qualify.

The discussions on the novel, the short story, poetry, and drama were based on extracts from works in English and hence they excluded the main body of work in Swahili, Zulu, Yoruba, Arabic, Amharic and other African languages. Yet, despite this exclusion of writers and literature in African languages, no sooner were the introductory preliminaries over than this Conference of 'African Writers of English Expression' sat down to the first item on the agenda:.'What is African Literature?'

The debate which followed was animated: Was it literature about Africa or about the African experience? Was it literature written by Africans? What about a non-African who wrote about Africa: did his work qualify as African literature? What if an African set his work in Greenland: did that qualify as African literature? Or were African languages the criteria? OK: what about Arabic, was it not foreign to Africa? What about French and English, which had become African languages? What if an European wrote about Europe in an African language? If ... if ... if ... this or that, except the issue: the domination of our languages and cultures by those of imperialist Europe: in any case there was no Fagunwa or Shabaan Robert or any writer in African languages to bring the conference down from the realms of evasive abstractions. The question was never seriously asked: did what we wrote qualify as African literature? The whole area of literature and audience, and hence of language as a determinant of both the national and class audience, did not really figure: the debate was more about the subject matter and the racial origins and geographical habitation of the writer.

English, like French and Portuguese, was assumed to be the natural language of literary and even political mediation between African people in the same nation and between nations in Africa and other continents. In some instances these European languages were seen as having a capacity to unite African peoples against divisive tendencies inherent in the multiplicity of African languages within the same geographic state. Thus Ezekiel Mphahlele later could write, in a letter to *Transition* number 11, that English and French have become the common language with which to present a nationalist front against white oppressors, and even 'where the whiteman has already retreated, as in the independent states, these two languages are still a unifying force'.[3] In the literary sphere they were often seen as coming to save African languages against themselves. Writing a foreword to Birago Diop's book *Contes d'Amadou Koumba* Sédar Senghor commends him for using French to rescue the spirit and style of old African fables and tales. 'However while rendering them into French he renews them with an art which, while it respects the genius of the French language, that language of gentleness and honesty, preserves at the same time all the virtues of the negro-african languages.'[4] English, French and Portuguese had come to our rescue and we accepted the unsolicited gift with gratitude. Thus in 1964, Chinua Achebe, in a speech entitled 'The African Writer and the English Language', said:

> Is it right that a man should abandon his mother tongue for someone else's? It looks like a dreadful betrayal and produces a guilty feeling. But for me there is no other choice. I have been given the language and I intend to use it.[5]

See the paradox: the possibility of using mother-tongues provokes a tone of levity in phrases like 'a dreadful betrayal' and 'a guilty feeling'; but that of foreign languages produces a categorical positive embrace, what Achebe himself, ten years later, was to describe as this 'fatalistic logic of the unassailable position of English in our literature'.[6]

The fact is that all of us who opted for European languages – the conference participants and the generation that followed them – accepted that fatalistic logic to a greater or lesser degree. We were guided by it and the only question which preoccupied us was how best to make the borrowed tongues carry the weight of our African experience by, for instance, making them 'prey' on African proverbs and other pecularities of African speech and folklore. For this task, Achebe (*Things Fall Apart*; *Arrow of God*), Amos Tutuola (*The Palm-wine Drinkard*; *My life in the Bush of Ghosts*), and Gabriel Okara (*The Voice*) were often held as providing the three alternative models. The lengths to which we were prepared to go in our mission of enriching foreign languages by injecting Senghorian 'black blood' into their rusty joints, is best exemplified by Gabriel Okara in an article reprinted in *Transition*:

As a writer who believes in the utilization of African ideas, African philosophy and African folklore and imagery to the fullest extent possible, I am of the opinion the only way to use them effectively is to translate them almost literally from the African language native to the writer into whatever European language he is using as medium of expression. I have endeavoured in my words to keep as close as possible to the vernacular expressions. For, from a word, a group of words, a sentence and even a name in any African language, one can glean the social norms, attitudes and values of a people.

In order to capture the vivid images of African speech, I had to eschew the habit of expressing my thoughts first in English. It was difficult at first, but I had to learn. I had to study each Ijaw expression I used and to discover the probable situation in which it was used in order to bring out the nearest meaning in English. I found it a fascinating exercise.[7]

Why, we may ask, should an African writer, or any writer, become so obsessed by taking from his mother-tongue to enrich other tongues? Why should he see it as his particular mission? We never asked ourselves: how can we enrich our languages? How can we 'prey' on the rich humanist and democratic heritage in the struggles of other peoples in other times and other places to enrich our own? Why not have Balzac, Tolstoy, Sholokov, Brecht, Lu Hsun, Pablo Neruda, H. C. Anderson, Kim Chi Ha, Marx, Lenin, Albert Einstein, Galileo, Aeschylus, Aristotle and Plato in African languages? And why not create literary monuments in our own languages? Why in other words should Okara not sweat it out to create in Ijaw, which he acknowledges to have depths of philosophy and a wide range of ideas and experiences? What was our responsibility to the struggles of African peoples? No, these questions were not asked. What seemed to worry us more was this: after all the literary gymnastics of preying on our languages to add life and vigour to English and other foreign languages, would the result be accepted as good English or good French? Will the owner of the language criticise our usage? Here we were more assertive of our rights! Chinua Achebe wrote:

I feel that the English language will be able to carry the weight of my African experience. But it will have to be a new English, still in full communion with its ancestral home but altered to suit new African surroundings.[8]

Gabriel Okara's position on this was representative of our generation:

> Some may regard this way of writing English as a desecration of the language. This is of course not true. Living languages grow like living things, and English is far from a dead language. There are American, West Indian, Australian, Canadian and New Zealand versions of English. All of them add life and vigour to the language while reflecting their own respective cultures. Why shouldn't there be a Nigerian or West African English which we can use to express our own ideas, thinking and philosophy in our own way?[9]

How did we arrive at this acceptance of 'the fatalistic logic of the unassailable position of English in our literature', in our culture and in our politics? What was the route from the Berlin of 1884 via the Makerere of 1962 to what is still the prevailing and dominant logic a hundred years later? How did we, as African writers, come to be so feeble towards the claims of our languages on us and so aggressive in our claims on other languages, particularly the languages of our colonization?

Berlin of 1884 was effected through the sword and the bullet. But the night of the sword and the bullet was followed by the morning of the chalk and the blackboard. The physical violence of the battlefield was followed by the psychological violence of the classroom. But where the former was visibly brutal, the latter was visibly gentle, a process best described in Cheikh Hamidou Kane's novel *Ambiguous Adventure* where he talks of the methods of the colonial phase of imperialism as consisting of knowing how to kill with efficiency and to heal with the same art.

> On the Black Continent, one began to understand that their real power resided not at all in the cannons of the first morning but in what followed the cannons. Therefore behind the cannons was the new school. The new school had the nature of both the cannon and the magnet. From the cannon it took the efficiency of a fighting weapon. But better than the cannon it made the conquest permanent. The cannon forces the body and the school fascinates the soul.[10]

In my view language was the most important vehicle through which that power fascinated and held the soul prisoner. The bullet was the means of the physical subjugation. Language was the means of the spiritual subjugation. Let me illustrate this by drawing upon experiences in my own education, particularly in language and literature.

9

III

I was born into a large peasant family: father, four wives and about twenty-eight children. I also belonged, as we all did in those days, to a wider extended family and to the community as a whole.

We spoke Gĩkũyũ as we worked in the fields. We spoke Gĩkũyũ in and outside the home. I can vividly recall those evenings of story-telling around the fireside. It was mostly the grown-ups telling the children but everybody was interested and involved. We children would re-tell the stories the following day to other children who worked in the fields picking the pyrethrum flowers, tea-leaves or coffee beans of our European and African landlords.

The stories, with mostly animals as the main characters, were all told in Gĩkũyũ. Hare, being small, weak but full of innovative wit and cunning, was our hero. We identified with him as he struggled against the brutes of prey like lion, leopard, hyena. His victories were our victories and we learnt that the apparently weak can outwit the strong. We followed the animals in their struggle against hostile nature – drought, rain, sun, wind – a confrontation often forcing them to search for forms of co-operation. But we were also interested in their struggles amongst themselves, and particularly between the beasts and the victims of prey. These twin struggles, against nature and other animals, reflected real-life struggles in the human world.

Not that we neglected stories with human beings as the main characters. There were two types of characters in such human-centred narratives: the species of truly human beings with qualities of courage, kindness, mercy, hatred of evil, concern for others; and a man-eat-man two-mouthed species with qualities of greed, selfishness, individualism and hatred of what was good for the larger co-operative community. Co-operation as the ultimate good in a community was a constant theme. It could unite human beings with animals against ogres and beasts of prey, as in the story of how dove, after being fed with castor-oil seeds, was sent to fetch a smith working far away from home and whose pregnant wife was being threatened by these man-eating two-mouthed ogres.

There were good and bad story-tellers. A good one could tell the same story over and over again, and it would always be fresh to us, the listeners. He or she could tell a story told by someone else and make it more alive and dramatic. The differences really were in the use of words and images and the inflexion of voices to effect different tones.

We therefore learnt to value words for their meaning and nuances. Language was not a mere string of words. It had a suggestive power well beyond the immediate and lexical meaning. Our appreciation of the suggestive magical power of language was reinforced by the games we played with words through riddles, proverbs, transpositions of syllables, or through nonsensical but musically arranged words.[11] So we learnt the music of our language on top of the content. The language, through images and symbols, gave us a view of the world, but it had a beauty of its own. The home and the field were then our pre-primary school but what is important, for this discussion, is that the language of our evening teach-ins, and the language of our immediate and wider community, and the language of our work in the fields were one.

And then I went to school, a colonial school, and this harmony was broken. The language of my education was no longer the language of my culture. I first went to Kamaandura, missionary run, and then to another called Maanguuū run by nationalists grouped around the Gĩkũyũ Independent and Karinga Schools Association. Our language of education was still Gĩkũyũ. The very first time I was ever given an ovation for my writing was over a composition in Gĩkũyũ. So for my first four years there was still harmony between the language of my formal education and that of the Limuru peasant community.

It was after the declaration of a state of emergency over Kenya in 1952 that all the schools run by patriotic nationalists were taken over by the colonial regime and were placed under District Education Boards chaired by Englishmen. English became the language of my formal education. In Kenya, English became more than a language: it was *the* language, and all the others had to bow before it in deference.

Thus one of the most humiliating experiences was to be caught speaking Gĩkũyũ in the vicinity of the school. The culprit was given corporal punishment – three to five strokes of the cane on bare buttocks – or was made to carry a metal plate around the neck with inscriptions such as I AM STUPID or I AM A DONKEY. Sometimes the culprits were fined money they could hardly afford. And how did the teachers catch the culprits? A button was initially given to one pupil who was supposed to hand it over to whoever was caught speaking his mother tongue. Whoever had the button at the end of the day would sing who had given it to him and the ensuing process would bring out all the culprits of the day. Thus children were turned into witch-hunters and in the process were being taught the lucrative value of being a traitor to one's immediate community.

The attitude to English was the exact opposite: any achievement in spoken or written English was highly rewarded; prizes, prestige, applause; the ticket to higher realms. English became the measure of intelligence and ability in the arts, the sciences, and all the other branches of learning. English became *the* main determinant of a child's progress up the ladder of formal education.

As you may know, the colonial system of education in addition to its apartheid racial demarcation had the structure of a pyramid: a broad primary base, a narrowing secondary middle, and an even narrower university apex. Selections from primary into secondary were through an examination, in my time called Kenya African Preliminary Examination, in which one had to pass six subjects ranging from Maths to Nature Study and Kiswahili. All the papers were written in English. Nobody could pass the exam who failed the English language paper no matter how brilliantly he had done in the other subjects. I remember one boy in my class of 1954 who had distinctions in all subjects except English, which he had failed. He was made to fail the entire exam. He went on to become a turn boy in a bus company. I who had only passes but a credit in English got a place at the Alliance High School, one of the most elitist institutions for Africans in colonial Kenya. The requirements for a place at the University, Makerere University College, were broadly the same: nobody could go on to wear the undergraduate red gown, no matter how brilliantly they had performed in all the other subjects unless they had a credit – not even a simple pass! – in English. Thus the most coveted place in the pyramid and in the system was only available to the holder of an English language credit card. English was the official vehicle and the magic formula to colonial elitedom.

Literary education was now determined by the dominant language while also reinforcing that dominance. Orature (oral literature) in Kenyan languages stopped. In primary school I now read simplified Dickens and Stevenson alongside Rider Haggard. Jim Hawkins, Oliver Twist, Tom Brown – not Hare, Leopard and Lion – were now my daily companions in the world of imagination. In secondary school, Scott and G. B. Shaw vied with more Rider Haggard, John Buchan, Alan Paton, Captain W. E. Johns. At Makerere I read English: from Chaucer to T. S. Eliot with a touch of Graham Greene.

Thus language and literature were taking us further and further from ourselves to other selves, from our world to other worlds.'

What was the colonial system doing to us Kenyan children? What were the consequences of, on the one hand, this systematic suppression of our languages and the literature they carried, and on the other the elevation of English and the literature it carried? To answer those questions, let me first examine the relationship of language to human experience, human culture, and the human perception of reality.

IV

Language, any language, has a dual character: it is both a means of communication and a carrier of culture. Take English. It is spoken in Britain and in Sweden and Denmark. But for Swedish and Danish people English is only a means of communication with non-Scandinavians. It is not a carrier of their culture. For the British, and particularly the English, it is additionally, and inseparably from its use as a tool of communication, a carrier of their culture and history. Or take Swahili in East and Central Africa. It is widely used as a means of communication across many nationalities. But it is not the carrier of a culture and history of many of those nationalities. However in parts of Kenya and Tanzania, and particularly in Zanzibar, Swahili is inseparably both a means of communication and a carrier of the culture of those people to whom it is a mother-tongue.

Language as communication has three aspects or elements. There is first what Karl Marx once called the language of real life,[12] the element basic to the whole notion of language, its origins and development: that is, the relations people enter into with one another in the labour process, the links they necessarily establish among themselves in the act of a people, a community of human beings, producing wealth or means of life like food, clothing, houses. A human community really starts its historical being as a community of co-operation in production through the division of labour; the simplest is between man, woman and child within a household; the more complex divisions are between branches of production such as those who are sole hunters, sole gatherers of fruits or sole workers in metal. Then there are the most complex divisions such as those in modern factories where a single product, say a shirt or a shoe, is the result of many hands and minds. Production is co-operation, is communication, is language, is expression of a relation between human beings and it is specifically human.

The second aspect of language as communication is speech and it imitates the language of real life, that is communication in production.

The verbal signposts both reflect and aid communication or the relations established between human beings in the production of their means of life. Language as a system of verbal signposts makes that production possible. The spoken word is to relations between human beings what the hand is to the relations between human beings and nature. The hand through tools mediates between human beings and nature and forms the language of real life: spoken words mediate between human beings and form the language of speech.

The third aspect is the written signs. The written word imitates the spoken. Where the first two aspects of language as communication through the hand and the spoken word historically evolved more or less simultaneously, the written aspect is a much later historical development. Writing is representation of sounds with visual symbols, from the simplest knot among shepherds to tell the number in a herd or the hieroglyphics among the Agĩkũyũ gicaandi singers and poets of Kenya, to the most complicated and different letter and picture writing systems of the world today.

In most societies the written and the spoken languages are the same, in that they represent each other: what is on paper can be read to another person and be received as that language which the recipient has grown up speaking. In such a society there is broad harmony for a child between the three aspects of language as communication. His interaction with nature and with other men is expressed in written and spoken symbols or signs which are both a result of that double interaction and a reflection of it. The association of the child's sensibility is with the language of his experience of life.

But there is more to it: communication between human beings is also the basis and process of evolving culture. In doing similar kinds of things and actions over and over again under similar circumstances, similar even in their mutability, certain patterns, moves, rhythms, habits, attitudes, experiences and knowledge emerge. Those experiences are handed over to the next generation and become the inherited basis for their further actions on nature and on themselves. There is a gradual accumulation of values which in time become almost self-evident truths governing their conception of what is right and wrong, good and bad, beautiful and ugly, courageous and cowardly, generous and mean in their internal and external relations. Over a time this becomes a way of life distinguishable from other ways of life. They develop a distinctive culture and history. Culture embodies those moral, ethical and aesthetic values, the set of spiritual eyeglasses, through which they come to view themselves and their place in the

14

universe. Values are the basis of a people's identity, their sense of particularity as members of the human race. All this is carried by language. Language as culture is the collective memory bank of a people's experience in history. Culture is almost indistinguishable from the language that makes possible its genesis, growth, banking, articulation and indeed its transmission from one generation to the next.

Language as culture also has three important aspects. Culture is a product of the history which it in turn reflects. Culture in other words is a product and a reflection of human beings communicating with one another in the very struggle to create wealth and to control it. But culture does not merely reflect that history, or rather it does so by actually forming images or pictures of the world of nature and nurture. Thus the second aspect of language as culture is as an image-forming agent in the mind of a child. Our whole conception of ourselves as a people, individually and collectively, is based on those pictures and images which may or may not correctly correspond to the actual reality of the struggles with nature and nurture which produced them in the first place. But our capacity to confront the world creatively is dependent on how those images correspond or not to that reality, how they distort or clarify the reality of our struggles. Language as culture is thus mediating between me and my own self; between my own self and other selves; between me and nature. Language is mediating in my very being. And this brings us to the third aspect of language as culture. Culture transmits or imparts those images of the world and reality through the spoken and the written language, that is through a specific language. In other words, the capacity to speak, the capacity to order sounds in a manner that makes for mutual comprehension between human beings is universal. This is the universality of language, a quality specific to human beings. It corresponds to the universality of the struggle against nature and that between human beings. But the particularity of the sounds, the words, the word order into phrases and sentences, and the specific manner, or laws, of their ordering is what distinguishes one language from another. Thus a specific culture is not transmitted through language in its universality but in its particularity as the language of a specific community with a specific history. Written literature and orature are the main means by which a particular language transmits the images of the world contained in the culture it carries.

Language as communication and as culture are then products of each other. Communication creates culture: culture is a means of

15

communication. Language carries culture, and culture carries, particularly through orature and literature, the entire body of values by which we come to perceive ourselves and our place in the world. How people perceive themselves affects how they look at their culture, at their politics and at the social production of wealth, at their entire relationship to nature and to other beings. Language is thus inseparable from ourselves as a community of human beings with a specific form and character, a specific history, a specific relationship to the world.

V

So what was the colonialist imposition of a foreign language doing to us children?

The real aim of colonialism was to control the people's wealth: what they produced, how they produced it, and how it was distributed; to control, in other words, the entire realm of the language of real life. Colonialism imposed its control of the social production of wealth through military conquest and subsequent political dictatorship. But its most important area of domination was the mental universe of the colonised, the control, through culture, of how people perceived themselves and their relationship to the world. Economic and political control can never be complete or effective without mental control. To control a people's culture is to control their tools of self-definition in relationship to others.

For colonialism this involved two aspects of the same process: the destruction or the deliberate undervaluing of a people's culture, their art, dances, religions, history, geography, education, orature and literature, and the conscious elevation of the language of the coloniser. The domination of a people's language by the languages of the colonising nations was crucial to the domination of the mental universe of the colonised.

Take language as communication. Imposing a foreign language, and suppressing the native languages as spoken and written, were already breaking the harmony previously existing between the African child and the three aspects of language. Since the new language as a means of communication was a product of and was reflecting the 'real language of life' elsewhere, it could never as spoken or written properly reflect or imitate the real life of that community. This may in part explain why technology always appears to us as slightly external, *their* product and not *ours*. The word 'missile' used to hold an alien far-away sound until I recently learnt its equivalent in Gĩkũyũ, *ngurukuhĩ*, and it made me apprehend it differently. Learning, for a colonial child, became a cerebral activity and not an emotionally felt experience.

But since the new, imposed languages could never completely break the native languages as spoken, their most effective area of domination was the third aspect of language as communication, the written. The language of an African child's formal education was foreign. The language of the books he read was foreign. The language of his conceptualisation was foreign. Thought, in him, took the visible form of a foreign language. So the written language of a child's upbringing in the school (even his spoken language within the school compound) became divorced from his spoken language at home. There was often not the slightest relationship between the child's written world, which was also the language of his schooling, and the world of his immediate environment in the family and the community. For a colonial child, the harmony existing between the three aspects of language as communication was irrevocably broken. This resulted in the disassociation of the sensibility of that child from his natural and social environment, what we might call colonial alienation. The alienation became reinforced in the teaching of history, geography, music, where bourgeois Europe was always the centre of the universe.

This disassociation, divorce, or alienation from the immediate environment becomes clearer when you look at colonial language as a carrier of culture.

Since culture is a product of the history of a people which it in turn reflects, the child was now being exposed exclusively to a culture that was a product of a world external to himself. He was being made to stand outside himself to look at himself. *Catching Them Young* is the title of a book on racism, class, sex, and politics in children's literature by Bob Dixon. 'Catching them young' as an aim was even more true of a colonial child. The images of this world and his place in it implanted in a child take years to eradicate, if they ever can be.

Since culture does not just reflect the world in images but actually, through those very images, conditions a child to see that world in a certain way, the colonial child was made to see the world and where he stands in it as seen and defined by or reflected in the culture of the language of imposition.

And since those images are mostly passed on through orature and literature it meant the child would now only see the world as seen in the literature of his language of adoption. From the point of view of alienation, that is of seeing oneself from outside oneself as if one was another self, it does not matter that the imported literature carried the great humanist tradition of the best in Shakespeare, Goethe, Balzac, Tolstoy, Gorky, Brecht, Sholokhov, Dickens. The location of this great mirror of imagination was necessarily Europe and its history and culture and the rest of the universe was seen from that centre.

But obviously it was worse when the colonial child was exposed to images of his world as mirrored in the written languages of his coloniser. Where his own native languages were associated in his impressionable mind with low status, humiliation, corporal punishment, slow-footed intelligence and ability or downright stupidity, non-intelligibility and barbarism, this was reinforced by the world he met in the works of such geniuses of racism as a Rider Haggard or a Nicholas Monsarrat; not to mention the pronouncement of some of the giants of western intellectual and political establishment, such as Hume ('. . . the negro is naturally inferior to the whites . . .'),[13] Thomas Jefferson ('. . . the blacks . . . are inferior to the whites on the endowments of both body and mind . . .'),[14] or Hegel with his Africa comparable to a land of childhood still enveloped in the dark mantle of the night as far as the development of self-conscious history was concerned. Hegel's statement that there was nothing harmonious with humanity to be found in the African character is representative of the racist images of Africans and Africa such a colonial child was bound to encounter in the literature of the colonial languages.[15] The results could be disastrous.

In her paper read to the conference on the teaching of African literature in schools held in Nairobi in 1973, entitled 'Written Literature and Black Images',[16] the Kenyan writer and scholar Professor Mĩcere Mũgo related how a reading of the description of Gagool as an old African woman in Rider Haggard's *King Solomon's Mines* had for a long time made her feel mortal terror whenever she encountered old African women. In his autobiography *This Life* Sydney Poitier describes how, as a result of the literature he had read, he had come to associate Africa with snakes. So on arrival in Africa and being put up in a modern hotel in a modern city, he could not sleep because he kept on looking for snakes everywhere, even under the bed. These two have been able to pinpoint the origins of their fears. But for most others the negative image becomes internalised and it affects their cultural and even political choices in ordinary living.

Thus Léopold Sédar Senghor has said very clearly that although the colonial language had been forced upon him, if he had been given the choice he would still have opted for French. He becomes lyrical in his subservience to French:

> We express ourselves in French since French has a universal vocation and since our message is also addressed to French people and others. In our languages [i.e. African languages] the halo that surrounds the words is by nature merely that of sap and blood; French words send out thousands of rays like diamonds.[17]

Senghor has now been rewarded by being anointed to an honoured place in the French Academy – that institution for safe-guarding the purity of the French language.

In Malawi, Banda has erected his own monument by way of an institution, The Kamuzu Academy, designed to aid the brightest pupils of Malawi in their mastery of English.

> It is a grammar school designed to produce boys and girls who will be sent to universities like Harvard, Chicago, Oxford, Cambridge and Edinburgh and be able to compete on equal terms with others elsewhere.
>
> The President has instructed that Latin should occupy a central place in the curriculum. All teachers must have had at least some Latin in their academic background. Dr Banda has often said that no one can fully master English without knowledge of languages such as Latin and French . . .[18]

For good measure no Malawian is allowed to teach at the academy – none is good enough – and all the teaching staff has been recruited from Britain. A Malawian might lower the standards, or rather, the purity of the English language. Can you get a more telling example of hatred of what is national, and a servile worship of what is foreign even though dead?

In history books and popular commentaries on Africa, too much has been made of the supposed differences in the policies of the various colonial powers, the British indirect rule (or the pragmatism of the British in their lack of a cultural programme!) and the French and Portuguese conscious programme of cultural assimilation. These are a matter of detail and emphasis. The final effect was the same: Senghor's embrace of French as this language with a universal vocation is not so different from Chinua Achebe's gratitude in 1964 to English – 'those of us who have inherited the English language may not be in a position to appreciate the value of the inheritance'.[19] The assumptions behind the practice of those of us who have abandoned our mother-tongues and adopted European ones as the creative vehicles of our imagination, are not different either.

Thus the 1962 conference of 'African Writers of English expression' was only recognising, with approval and pride of course, what through all the years of selective education and rigorous tutelage, we had already been led to accept: the 'fatalistic logic of the unassailable position of English in our literature'. The logic was embodied deep in imperialism; and it was imperialism and its effects that we did not examine at Makerere. It is the final triumph of a system of domination when the dominated start singing its virtues.

VI

The twenty years that followed the Makerere conference gave the world a unique literature – novels, stories, poems, plays written by Africans in European languages – which soon consolidated itself into a tradition with companion studies and a scholarly industry.

Right from its conception it was the literature of the petty-bourgeoisie born of the colonial schools and universities. It could not be otherwise, given the linguistic medium of its message. Its rise and development reflected the gradual accession of this class to political and even economic dominance. But the petty-bourgeoisie in Africa was a large class with different strands in it. It ranged from that section which looked forward to a permanent alliance with imperialism in which it played the role of an intermediary between the bourgeoisie of the western metropolis and the people of the colonies – the section which in my book *Detained: A Writer's Prison Diary* I have described as the comprador bourgeoisie – to that section which saw the future in terms of a vigorous independent national economy in African capitalism or in some kind of socialism, what I shall here call the nationalistic or patriotic bourgeoisie. This literature by Africans in European languages was specifically that of the nationalistic bourgeoisie in its creators, its thematic concerns and its consumption.[20]

Internationally the literature helped this class, which in politics, business, and education, was assuming leadership of the countries newly emergent from colonialism, or of those struggling to so emerge, to explain Africa to the world: Africa had a past and a culture of dignity and human complexity.

Internally the literature gave this class a cohesive tradition and a common literary frame of references, which it otherwise lacked with its uneasy roots in the culture of the peasantry and in the culture of the metropolitan bourgeoisie. The literature added confidence to the class: the petty-bourgeoisie now had a past, a culture and a literature with which to confront the racist bigotry of Europe. This confidence – manifested in the tone of the writing, its sharp critique of European bourgeois civilisation, its implications, particularly in its negritude mould, that Africa had something new to give to the world — reflects the political ascendancy of the patriotic nationalistic section of the petty-bourgeoisie before and immediately after independence.

So initially this literature – in the post-war world of national democratic revolutionary and anti-colonial liberation in China and India, armed uprisings in Kenya and Algeria, the independence of Ghana and Nigeria with others impending – was part of that great anti-colonial and anti-imperialist upheaval in Asia, Africa, Latin America and Caribbean islands. It was inspired by the general political awakening; it drew its stamina and even form from the peasantry: their proverbs, fables, stories, riddles, and wise sayings. It was shot through and through with optimism. But later, when the comprador section assumed political ascendancy and strengthened rather than weakened the economic links with imperialism in what was clearly a neo-colonial arrangement, this literature became more and more critical, cynical, disillusioned, bitter and denunciatory in tone. It was almost unanimous in its portrayal, with varying degrees of detail, emphasis, and clarity of vision, of the post-independence betrayal of hope. But to whom was it directing its list of mistakes made, crimes and wrongs committed, complaints unheeded, or its call for a change of moral direction? The imperialist bourgeoisie? The petty-bourgeoisie in power? The military, itself part and parcel of that class? It sought another audience, principally the peasantry and the working class or what was generally conceived as the people. The search for new audience and new directions was reflected in the quest for simpler forms, in the adoption of a more direct tone, and often in a direct call for action. It was also reflected in the content. Instead of seeing Africa as one undifferentiated mass of historically wronged blackness, it now attempted some sort of class analysis and evaluation of neo-colonial societies. But this search was still within the confines of the languages of Europe whose use it now defended with less vigour and confidence. So its quest was hampered by the very language choice, and in its movement toward the people, it could only go up to that section of the petty-bourgeoisie – the students, teachers, secretaries for instance – still in closest touch with the people. It settled there, marking time, caged within the linguistic fence of its colonial inheritance.

Its greatest weakness still lay where it has always been, in the audience – the petty-bourgeoisie readership automatically assumed by the very choice of language. Because of its indeterminate economic position between the many contending classes, the petty-bourgeoisie develops a vacillating psychological make-up. Like a chameleon it takes on the colour of the main class with which it is in the closest touch and sympathy. It can be swept to activity by the masses at a time of revolutionary tide; or be driven to silence, fear, cynicism, withdrawal into self-contemplation, existential anguish, or to collaboration with the powers-that-be at times of reactionary tides. In African this class has always oscillated between the imperialist bourgeoisie and its comprador neo-colonial ruling elements on the one hand, and the peasantry and the working class (the masses) on the other. This very lack of identity in its social and psychological make-up as a class, was reflected in the very literature it produced: the crisis of identity was assumed in that very preoccupation with definition at the Makerere conference. In literature as in politics it spoke as if its identity or the crisis of its own identity was that of society as a whole. The literature it produced in European languages was given the identity of African literature as if there had never been literature in African languages. Yet by avoiding a real confrontation with the language issue, it was clearly wearing false robes of identity: it was a pretender to the throne of the mainstream of African literature. The practitioner of what Janheinz Jahn called neo-African literature tried to get out of the dilemma by over-insisting that European languages were really African languages or by trying to Africanise English or French usage while making sure it was still recognisable as English or French or Portuguese.

In the process this literature created, falsely and even absurdly, an English-speaking (or French or Portuguese) African peasantry and working class, a clear negation or falsification of the historical process and reality. This European-language-speaking peasantry and working class, existing only in novels and dramas, was at times invested with the vacillating mentality, the evasive self-contemplation, the existential anguished human condition, or the man-torn-between-two-worlds-facedness of the petty-bourgeoisie.

In fact, if it had been left entirely to this class, African languages would have ceased to exist – with independence!

VII

But African languages refused to die. They would not simply go the way of Latin to become the fossils for linguistic archaeology to dig up, classify, and argue about the international conferences.

These languages, these national heritages of Africa, were kept alive by the peasantry. The peasantry saw no contradiction between speaking their own mother-tongues and belonging to a larger national or continental geography. They saw no necessary antagonistic contradiction between belonging to their immediate nationality, to their multinational state along the Berlin-drawn boundaries, and to Africa as a whole. These people happily spoke Wolof, Hausa, Yoruba, Ibo, Arabic, Amharic, Kiswahili, Gĩkũyũ, Luo, Luhya, Shona, Ndebele, Kimbundu, Zulu or Lingala without this fact tearing the multinational states apart. During the anti-colonial struggle they showed an unlimited capacity to unite around whatever leader or party best and most consistently articulated an anti-imperialist position. If anything it was the petty-bourgeoisie, particularly the compradors, with their French and English and Portuguese, with their petty rivalries, their ethnic chauvinism, which encouraged these vertical divisions to the point of war at times. No, the peasantry had no complexes about their languages and the cultures they carried!

In fact when the peasantry and the working class were compelled by necessity or history to adopt the language of the master, they Africanised it without any of the respect for its ancestry shown by Senghor and Achebe, so totally as to have created new African languages, like Krio in Sierra Leone or Pidgin in Nigeria, that owed their identities to the syntax and rhythms of African languages. All these languages were kept alive in the daily speech, in the ceremonies, in political struggles, above all in the rich store of orature – proverbs, stories, poems, and riddles.

The peasantry and the urban working class threw up singers. These sang the old songs or composed new ones incorporating the new experiences in industries and urban life and in working-class struggle and organisations. These singers pushed the languages to new limits, renewing and reinvigorating them by coining new words and new expressions, and in generally expanding their capacity to incorporate new happenings in Africa and the world.

The peasantry and the working class threw up their own writers, or attracted to their ranks and concern intellectuals from among the

23

petty-bourgeoisie, who all wrote in African languages. It is these writers like Heruy Wäldä Sellassie, Germacäw Takla Hawaryat, Shabaan Robert, Abdullatif Abdalla, Ebrahim Hussein, Euphrase Kezilahabi, B. H. Vilakazi, Okot p'Bitek, A. C. Jordan, P. Mboya, D. O. Fagunwa, Mazisi Kunene and many others rightly celebrated in Albert Gérard's pioneering survey of literature in African languages from the tenth century to the present, called *African Language Literatures* (1981), who have given our languages a written literature. Thus the immortality of our languages in print has been ensured despite the internal and external pressures for their extinction. In Kenya I would like to single out Gakaara wa Wanjaū, who was jailed by the British for the ten years between 1952 and 1962 because of his writing in Gĩkũyũ. His book, *Mwandĩki wa Mau Mau Ithaamĩrioinĩ*, a diary he secretly kept while in political detention, was published by Heinemann Kenya and won the 1984 Noma Award. It is a powerful work, extending the range of the Gĩkũyũ language prose, and it is a crowning achievement to the work he started in 1946. He has worked in poverty, in the hardships of prison, in post-independence isolation when the English language held sway in Kenya's schools from nursery to University and in every walk of the national printed world, but he never broke his faith in the possibilities of Kenya's national languages. His inspiration came from the mass anti-colonial movement of Kenyan people, particularly the militant wing grouped around Mau Mau or the Kenya Land and Freedom Army, which in 1952 ushered in the era of modern guerrilla warfare in Africa. He is the clearest example of those writers thrown up by the mass political movements of an awakened peasantry and working class.

And finally from among the European-language-speaking African petty-bourgeoisie, there emerged a few who refused to join the chorus of those who had accepted the 'fatalistic logic' of the position of European languages in our literary being. It was one of these, Obi Wali, who pulled the carpet from under the literary feet of those who gathered at Makerere in 1962 by declaring in an article published in *Transition* (10, September 1963), 'that the whole uncritical acceptance of English and French as the inevitable medium for educated African writing is misdirected, and has no chance of advancing African literature and culture', and that until African writers accepted that any true African literature must be written in African languages, they would merely be pursuing a dead end.

What we would like future conferences on African literature to devote time to, is the all-important problem of African writing in African languages, and all its implications for the development of a truly African sensibility.

Obi Wali had his predecessors. Indeed people like David Diop of Senegal had put the case against this use of colonial languages even more strongly.

> The African creator, deprived of the use of his language and cut off from his people, might turn out to be only the representative of a literary trend (and that not necessarily the least gratuitous) of the conquering nation. His works, having become a perfect illustration of the assimilationist policy through imagination and style, will doubtless rouse the warm applause of a certain group of critics. In fact, these praises will go mostly to colonialism which, when it can no longer keep its subjects in slavery, transforms them into docile intellectuals patterned after Western literary fashions which besides, is another more subtle form of bastardization.[22]

David Diop quite correctly saw that the use of English and French was a matter of temporary historical necessity.

> Surely in an Africa freed from oppression it will not occur to any writer to express, otherwise than in his rediscovered language, his feelings and the feelings of his people.[23]

The importance of Obi Wali's intervention was in tone and timing: it was published soon after the 1962 Makerere conference of African writers of English expression; it was polemical and aggressive, poured ridicule and scorn on the choice of English and French, while being unapologetic in its call for the use of African languages. Not surprisingly it was met with hostility and then silence. But twenty years of uninterrupted dominance of literature in European languages, the reactionary turn that political and economic events in Africa have taken, and the search for a revolutionary break with the neo-colonial status quo, all compel soul-searching among writers, raising once again the entire question of the language of African literature.

VIII

The question is this: we as African writers have always complained about the neo-colonial economic and political relationship to Euro-America. Right. But by our continuing to write in foreign languages, paying homage to them, are we not on the cultural level continuing that neo-colonial slavish and cringing spirit? What is the difference between a politician who says Africa cannot do without imperialism and the writer who says Africa cannot do without European languages?

While we were busy haranguing the ruling circles in a language which automatically excluded the participation of the peasantry and the working class in the debate, imperialist culture and African reactionary forces had a field day: the Christian bible is available in unlimited quantities in even the tiniest African language. The comprador ruling cliques are also quite happy to have the peasantry and the working class all to themselves: distortions, dictatorial directives, decrees, museum-type fossils paraded as African culture, feudalistic ideologies, superstitions, lies, all these backward elements and more are communicated to the African masses in their own languages without any challenges from those with alternative visions of tomorrow who have deliberately cocooned themselves in English, French, and Portuguese. It is ironic that the most reactionary African politician, the one who believes in selling Africa to Europe, is often a master of African languages; that the most zealous of European missionaries who believed in rescuing Africa from itself, even from the paganism of its languages, were nevertheless masters of African languages, which they often reduced to writing. The European missionary believed too much in his mission of conquest not to communicate it in the languages most readily available to the people: the African writer believes too much in 'African literature' to write it in those ethnic, divisive and under-developed languages of the peasantry!

The added irony is that what they have produced, despite any claims to the contrary, is not African literature. The editors of the Pelican Guides to English literature in their latest volume were right to include a discussion of this literature as part of twentieth-century English literature, just as the French Academy was right to honour Senghor for his genuine and talented contribution to French literature and language. What we have created is another hybrid tradition, a tradition in transition, a minority tradition that can only be termed as Afro-

European literature; that is, the literature written by Africans in European languages.[24] It has produced many writers and works of genuine talent: Chinua Achebe, Wole Soyinka, Ayi Kwei Armah, Sembene Ousmane, Agostino Neto, Sédar Senghor and many others. Who can deny their talent? The light in the products of their fertile imaginations has certainly illuminated important aspects of the African being in its continuous struggle against the political and economic consequences of Berlin and after. However we cannot have our cake and eat it! Their work belongs to an Afro-European literary tradition which is likely to last for as long as Africa is under this rule of European capital in a neo-colonial set-up. So Afro-European literature can be defined as literature written by Africans in European languages in the era of imperialism.

But some are coming round to the inescapable conclusion articulated by Obi Wali with such polemical vigour twenty years ago: African literature can only be written in African languages, that is, the languages of the African peasantry and working class, the major alliance of classes in each of our nationalities and the agency for the coming inevitable revolutionary break with neo-colonialism.

IX

I started writing in Gĩkũyũ language in 1977 after seventeen years of involvement in Afro-European literature, in my case Afro-English literature. It was then that I collaborated with Ngũgĩ wa Mĩriĩ in the drafting of the playscript, *Ngaahika Ndeenda* (the English translation was *I Will Marry When I Want*). I have since published a novel in Gĩkũyũ, *Caitaani Mũtharabainĩ* (English translation: *Devil on the Cross*) and completed a musical drama, *Maitũ Njugĩra*, (English translation: *Mother Sing for Me*); three books for children, *Njamba Nene na Mbaathi i Mathagu*, *Bathitoora ya Njamba Nene*, *Njamba Nene na Cibũ Kĩng'ang'i*, as well as another novel manuscript: *Matigari Ma Njirũũngi*. Wherever I have gone, particularly in Europe, I have been confronted with the question: why are you now writing in Gĩkũyũ? Why do you now write in an African language? In some academic quarters I have been confronted with the rebuke, 'Why have you abandoned us?' It was almost as if, in choosing to write in Gĩkũyũ, I was doing something abnormal. But Gĩkũyũ is my mother tongue! The very fact that what common sense dictates in the literary practice

27

of other cultures is being questioned in an African writer is a measure of how far imperialism has distorted the view of African realities. It has turned reality upside down: the abnormal is viewed as normal and the normal is viewed as abnormal. Africa actually enriches Europe: but Africa is made to believe that it needs Europe to rescue it from poverty. Africa's natural and human resources continue to develop Europe and America: but Africa is made to feel grateful for aid from the same quarters that still sit on the back of the continent. Africa even produces intellectuals who now rationalise this upside-down way of looking at Africa.

I believe that my writing in Gĩkũyũ language, a Kenyan language, an African language, is part and parcel of the anti-imperialist struggles of Kenyan and African peoples. In schools and universities our Kenyan languages – that is the languages of the many nationalities which make up Kenya – were associated with negative qualities of backwardness, underdevelopment, humiliation and punishment. We who went through that school system were meant to graduate with a hatred of the people and the culture and the values of the language of our daily humiliation and punishment. I do not want to see Kenyan children growing up in that imperialist-imposed tradition of contempt for the tools of communication developed by their communities and their history. I want them to transcend colonial alienation.

Colonial alienation takes two interlinked forms: an active (or passive) distancing of oneself from the reality around; and an active (or passive) identification with that which is most external to one's environment. It starts with a deliberate disassociation of the language of conceptualisation, of thinking, of formal education, of mental development, from the language of daily interaction in the home and in the community. It is like separating the mind from the body so that they are occupying two unrelated linguistic spheres in the same person. On a larger social scale it is like producing a society of bodiless heads and headless bodies.

So I would like to contribute towards the restoration of the harmony between all the aspects and divisions of language so as to restore the Kenyan child to his environment, understand it fully so as to be in a position to change it for his collective good. I would like to see Kenya peoples' mother-tongues (our national languages!) carry a literature reflecting not only the rhythms of a child's spoken expression, but also his struggle with nature and his social nature. With that harmony between himself, his language and his environment as his starting point, he can learn other languages and even enjoy the positive humanistic, democratic and revolutionary elements in other people's literatures and cultures without any complexes about his own language, his own self, his environment. The all-Kenya national language (i.e. Kiswahili); the other national languages (i.e. the languages of the nationalities like Luo, Gīkūyū, Maasai, Luhya, Kallenjin, Kamba, Mijikenda, Somali, Galla, Turkana, Arabic-speaking people, etc.); other African languages like Hausa, Wolof, Yoruba, Ibo, Zulu, Nyanja, Lingala, Kimbundu; and foreign languages – that is foreign to Africa – like English, French, German, Russian, Chinese, Japanese, Portuguese, Spanish will fall into their proper perspective in the lives of Kenyan children.

Chinua Achebe once decried the tendency of African intellectuals to escape into abstract universalism in the words that apply even more to the issue of the language of African literature:

Africa has had such a fate in the world that the very adjective *African* can call up hideous fears of rejection. Better then to cut all the links with this homeland, this liability, and become in one giant leap the universal man. Indeed I understand this anxiety. *But running away from oneself seems to me a very inadequate way of dealing with an anxiety* [italics mine]. And if writers should opt for such escapism, who is to meet the challenge?[25]

Who indeed?

We African writers are bound by our calling to do for our languages what Spencer, Milton and Shakespeare did for English; what Pushkin and Tolstoy did for Russian; indeed what all writers in world history have done for their languages by meeting the challenge of creating a literature in them, which process later opens the languages for philosophy, science, technology and all the other areas of human creative endeavours.

But writing in our languages per se – although a necessary first step in the correct direction – will not itself bring about the renaissance in African cultures if that literature does not carry the content of our people's anti-imperialist struggles to liberate their productive forces from foreign control; the content of the need for unity among the workers and peasants of all the nationalities in their struggle to control the wealth they produce and to free it from internal and external parasites.

In other words writers in African languages should reconnect themselves to the revolutionary traditions of an organised peasantry and working class in Africa in their struggle to defeat imperialism and create a higher system of democracy and socialism in alliance with all the other peoples of the world. Unity in that struggle would ensure unity in our multi-lingual diversity. It would also reveal the real links that bind the people of Africa to the peoples of Asia, South America, Europe, Australia and New Zealand, Canada and the U.S.A.

But it is precisely when writers open out African languages to the real links in the struggles of peasants and workers that they will meet their biggest challenge. For to the comprador-ruling regimes, their real enemy is an awakened peasantry and working class. A writer who tries to communicate the message of revolutionary unity and hope in the languages of the people becomes a subversive character. It is then that writing in African languages becomes a subversive or treasonable offence with such a writer facing possibilities of prison, exile or even death. For him there are no 'national' accolades, no new year honours, only abuse and slander and innumerable lies from the mouths of the armed power of a ruling minority – ruling, that is, on behalf of U.S.-led imperialism – and who see in democracy a real threat. A democratic participation of the people in the shaping of their own lives or in discussing their own lives in languages that allow for mutual comprehension is seen as being dangerous to the good government of a country and its institutions. African languages addressing themselves to the lives of the people become the enemy of a neo-colonial state.

Notes

1 'European languages became so important to the Africans that they defined their own identities partly by reference to those languages. Africans began to describe each other in terms of being either Francophone or English-speaking Africans. The continent itself was thought of in terms of French-speaking states, English-speaking states and Arabic-speaking states.'
Ali A. Mazrui, *Africa's International Relations*, London: 1977, p. 92.
   Arabic does not quite fall into that category. Instead of Arabic-speaking states as an example, Mazrui should have put Portuguese-speaking states. Arabic is now an African language unless we want to write off all the indigenous populations of North Africa, Egypt, Sudan as not being Africans.
   And as usual with Mazrui his often apt and insightful descriptions, observations, and comparisons of the contemporary African realities as affected by Europe are, unfortunately, often tinged with approval or a sense of irreversible inevitability.
2 The conference was organized by the anti-Communist Paris-based but American-inspired and financed Society for Cultural Freedom which was later discovered actually to have been financed by CIA. It shows how certain directions in our cultural, political, and economic choices can be masterminded from the metropolitan centres of imperialism.
3 This is an argument often espoused by colonial spokesmen. Compare Mphahlele's comment with that of Geoffrey Moorhouse in *Manchester Guardian Weekly*, 15

July 1964, as quoted by Ali A. Mazrui and Michael Tidy in their work *Nationalism and New States in Africa*, London: 1984.

'On both sides of Africa, moreover, in Ghana and Nigeria, in Uganda and in Kenya, the spread of education has led to an increased demand for English at primary level. *The remarkable thing is that English has not been rejected as a symbol of Colonialism; it has rather been adopted as a politically neutral language beyond the reproaches of tribalism.* It is also a more attractive proposition in Africa than in either India or Malaysia because comparatively few Africans are completely literate in the vernacular tongues and even in the languages of regional communication, Hausa and Swahili, which are spoken by millions, and only read and written by thousands.' (My italics)

Is Moorehouse telling us that the English language is politically neutral vis-à-vis Africa's confrontation with neo-colonialism? Is he telling us that by 1964 there were more Africans literate in European languages than in African languages? That Africans could not, even if that was the case, be literate in their own national languages or in the regional languages? Really is Mr Moorehouse tongue-tying the African?

4　The English title is *Tales of Amadou Koumba*, published by Oxford University Press. The translation of this particular passage from the *Présence Africaine*, Paris edition of the book was done for me by Dr Bachir Diagne in Bayreuth.

5　The paper is now in Achebe's collection of essays *Morning Yet on Creation Day*, London: 1975.

6　In the introduction to *Morning Yet on Creation Day* Achebe obviously takes a slightly more critical stance from his 1964 position. The phrase is apt for a whole generation of us African writers.

7　*Transition* No. 10, September 1963, reprinted from *Dialogue*, Paris.

8　Chinua Achebe 'The African Writer and the English Language', in *Morning Yet on Creation Day*.

9　Gabriel Okara, *Transition* No. 10, September 1963.

10　Cheikh Hamidou Kane *L'aventure Ambiguë*. (English translation: *Ambiguous Adventure*). This passage was translated for me by Bachir Diagne.

11　Example from a tongue twister: 'Kaana ka Nikoora koona koora koora: na ko koora koona kaana ka Nikoora koora koora.' I'm indebted to Wangui wa Goro for this example. 'Nichola's child saw a baby frog and ran away: and when the baby frog saw Nichola's child it also ran away.' A Gĩkũyũ speaking child has to get the correct tone and length of vowel and pauses to get it right. Otherwise it becomes a jumble of *k*'s and *r*'s and *na*'s.

12　'The production of ideas, of conceptions, of consciousness, is at first directly interwoven with the material activity and the material intercourse of men, the language of real life. Conceiving, thinking, the mental intercourse of men, appear at this stage as the direct efflux of their material behaviour. The same applies to mental production as expressed in the language of politics, laws, morality, religion, metaphysics, etc., of a people. Men are the producers of their conceptions, ideas etc. – real, active men, as they are conditioned by a definite development of their productive forces and of the intercourse corresponding to these, up to its furthest form.' Marx and Engels, German Ideology, the first part published under the title, *Feuerbach: Opposition of the Materialist and Idealist Outlooks*, London: 1973, p. 8.

13　Quoted in Eric Williams *A History of the People of Trinidad and Tobago*, London 1964, p. 32.

14　Eric Williams, ibid., p. 31.

15　In references to Africa in the introduction to his lectures in *The Philosophy of History*, Hegel gives historical, philosophical, rational expression and legitimacy to every conceivable European racist myth about Africa. Africa is even denied her own geography where it does not correspond to the myth. Thus Egypt is not part of

Africa; and North Africa is part of Europe. Africa proper is the especial home of ravenous beasts, snakes of all kinds. The African is not part of humanity. Only slavery to Europe can raise him, possibly, to the lower ranks of humanity. Slavery is good for the African. 'Slavery is in and for itself *injustice*, for the essence of humanity is *freedom*; but for this man must be matured. The gradual abolition of slavery is therefore wiser and more equitable than its sudden removal.' (Hegel *The Philosophy of History*, Dover edition, New York: 1956, pp. 91–9.) Hegel clearly reveals himself as the nineteenth-century Hitler of the intellect.

16   The paper is now in Akivaga and Gachukiah's *The Teaching of African Literature in Schools*, published by Kenya Literature Bureau.

17   Senghor, Introduction to his poems, 'Éthiopiques, le 24 Septembre 1954', in answering the question: 'Pourquoi, dès lors, écrivez-vous en français?' Here is the whole passage in French. See how lyrical Senghor becomes as he talks of his encounter with French language and French literature.

Mais on me posera la question: 'Pourquoi, dès lors, écrivez-vous en français?' parce que nous sommes des métis culturels, parce que, si nous sentons en nègres, nous nous exprimons en français, parce que le français est une langue à vocation universelle, que notre message s'adresse *aussi* aux Français de France et aux autres hommes, parce que le français est une langue 'de gentillesse et d'honnêteté'. Qui a dit que c'était une langue grise et atone d'ingénieurs et de diplomates? Bien sûr, moi aussi, je l'ai dit un jour, pour les besoins de ma thèse. On me le pardonnera. Car je sais ses ressources pour l'avoir goûté, mâché, enseigné, et qu'il est la langue des dieux. Ecoutez donc Corneille, Lautréamont, Rimbaud, Péguy et Claudel. Écoutez le grand Hugo. Le français, ce sont les grandes orgues qui se prêtent à tous les timbres, à tous les effets, des douceurs les plus suaves aux fulgurances de l'orage. Il est, tour à tour ou en même temps, flûte, hautbois, trompette, tamtam et même canon. Et puis le français nous a fait don de ses mots abstraits – si rares dans nos langues maternelles –, où les larmes se font pierres précieuses. Chez nous, les mots sont naturellement nimbés d'un halo de sève et de sang; les mots du français rayonnent de mille feux, comme des diamants. Des fusées qui éclairent notre nuit.

See also Senghor's reply to a question on language in an interview by Armand Guiber and published in *Présence Africaine* 1962 under the title, Leópold Sédar Senghor:

Il est vrai que le français n'est pas ma langue maternelle. J'ai commencé de l'apprendre à sept ans, par des mots comme 'confitures' et 'chocolat'. Aujourd'-hui, je pense naturellement en Français, et je comprend le Français – faut-il en avoir honte? Mieux qu'aucune autre langue. C'est dire que le Français n'est plus pour moi un 'véhicule étranger' mais la forme d'expression naturelle de ma pensée.

Ce qui m'est étrange dans le français, c'est peut-être son style: Son architecture classique. Je suis naturellement porté à gonfler d'image son cadre étroit, sans la poussée de la chaleur émotionelle.

18   *Zimbabwe Herald* August 1981.

19   Chinua Achebe 'The African Writer and the English Language' in *Morning Yet on Creation Day* p. 59.

20   Most of the writers were from Universities. The readership was mainly the product of schools and colleges. As for the underlying theme of much of that literature, Achebe's statement in his paper, 'The Novelist as a Teacher', is instructive:
      'If I were God I would regard as the very worst our acceptance – for whatever reason – of racial inferiority. It is too late in the day to get worked up about it or to

blame others, much as they may deserve such blame and condemnation. What we need to do is to look back and try and find out where we went wrong, where the rain began to beat us.

'Here then is an adequate revolution for me to espouse – to help my society regain belief in itself and put away the complexes of the years of denigration and self-abasement.' *Morning Yet on Creation Day*, p. 44.

Since the peasant and the worker had never really had any doubts about their Africanness, the reference could only have been to the 'educated' or the petty-bourgeois African. In fact if one substitutes the words 'the petty-bourgeois' for the word 'our' and 'the petty-bourgeois class' for 'my society' the statement is apt, accurate, and describes well the assumed audience. Of course, an ideological revolution in this class would affect the whole society.

22 David Diop 'Contribution to the Debate on National Poetry', *Présence Africaine* 6, 1956.

23 David Diop, ibid.

24 The term 'Afro-European Literature' may seem to put too much weight on the Europeanness of the literature. Euro-African literature? Probably, the English, French, and Portuguese components would then be 'Anglo-African literature', 'Franco-African literature' or 'Luso-African literature'. What is important is that this minority literature forms a distinct tradition that needs a different term to distinguish it from *African Literature*, instead of usurping the title *African Literature* as is the current practice in literary scholarship. There have even been arrogant claims by some literary scholars who talk as if the literature written in European languages is necessarily closer to the Africanness of its inspiration than similar works in African languages, the languages of the majority. So thoroughly has the minority 'Afro-European Literature' (Euro-African literature?) usurped the name 'African literature' in the current scholarship that literature by Africans in African languages is the one that needs qualification. Albert Gérard's otherwise timely book is titled *African Language Literatures*.

25 Chinua Achebe 'Africa and her Writers' in *Morning Yet on Creation Day*, p. 27.

2 The Language of African Theatre

I

Early one morning in 1976, a woman from Kamĩrĩĩthũ village came to my house and she went straight to the point: 'We hear you have a lot of education and that you write books. Why don't you and others of your kind give some of that education to the village? We don't want the whole amount; just a little of it, and a little of your time.' There was a youth centre in the village, she went on, and it was falling apart. It needed group effort to bring it back to life. Would I be willing to help? I said I would think about it. In those days, I was the chairman of the Literature Department at the University of Nairobi but I lived near Kamĩrĩĩthũ, Limuru, about thirty or so kilometres from the capital city. I used to drive to Nairobi and back daily except on Sundays. So Sunday was the best day to catch me at home. She came the second, the third and the fourth consecutive Sundays with the same request couched in virtually the same words. That was how I came to join others in what later was to be called Kamĩrĩĩthũ Community Education and Cultural Centre.

II

Kamĩrĩĩthũ is one of several villages in Limuru originally set up in the fifties by the British colonial administration as a way of cutting off the links between the people and the guerrillas of the Kenya Land and Freedom Army, otherwise known as Mau Mau. Even after independence in 1963 the villages remained as reservoirs of cheap labour. By 1975 Kamĩrĩĩthũ alone had grown into a population of ten thousand. The workers who live in Kamĩrĩĩthũ, either as rent-paying tenants or as owners, fall into three broad categories. Firstly there are those who work at Bata, the multinational shoe-making factory, at the Nile Investments Plastic Pipes and Goods factory, at the small salt-processing plants, at the timber and maize mills and at the motor and bicycle repairing garages – all part of a growing industrial proletariat. Then there are those employed in hotels, shops, petrol stations, transport buses and matatus, with donkey-pulled carriages and human-powered pushçarts – commercial and domestic workers. The third category are part of the agricultural proletariat; those who are mainly employed in the huge tea and coffee plantations and farms previously owned by the British colonial settlers but which now belong to a few wealthy Kenyans and multinationals like Lonrho, but also those who are employed as seasonal labour on farms of all sizes.

But the peasants are the majority. They include 'rich' peasants who employ more than family labour; middle peasants who depend solely on family labour; poor peasants who work on their own strips of land but also hire out their labour; and numerous landless peasants who rent land and hire out themselves. There are of course the many unemployed, plus part-time and full-time prostitutes and petty criminals. The other distinct type of dwellers in Kamīrīīthū are teachers, secretaries, petty administrative officials, owners of small bars and shops, self-employed craftsmen, carpenters, musicians, market traders, and the occasional businessman – that is, the petty bourgeoisie. Most of the rich landlords, merchants, and top officials in companies or administration, and a large section of the land-owning peasantry, live outside the village.[1]

I mention these different classes because nearly all of them were represented among the participants at Kamīrīīthū Community Education and Culture Centre. For instance, the committee running the centre was made up of peasants, workers, a schoolteacher and a businessman. Those of us from the University included Kīmani, Gecaū, Kabirū Kinyanjui and Ngūgī wa Mīriī who later became the co-ordinating director of all our activities. But the peasants and the workers, including the unemployed, were the real backbone of the centre which started functioning in 1976.

I have talked about the origins, the aims, and the development of the centre in my books, *Detained: A Writer's Prison Diary* and *Barrel of a Pen: Resistance to Repression in Neo-colonial Kenya*, and in various other publications. A great deal has also been written about it in newspapers, journals and research papers. But what is important, for our discussion on the language of African theatre, is that all the activities of the centre were to be linked – they would arise out of each other – while each being a self-contained programme. Thus *theatre*, as the central focus of our cultural programme, was going to provide follow-up material and activities for the new literates from the adult literacy programme, while at the same time providing the basis for polytechnic type activities in the material culture programme.

But why theatre in the village? Were we introducing something totally alien to the community as the Provincial Commissioner was later to claim?

III

Drama has origins in human struggles with nature and with others. In pre-colonial Kenya, the peasants in the various nationalities cleared forests, planted crops, tended them to ripeness and harvest – out of the one seed buried in the ground came many seeds. Out of death life sprouted, and this through the mediation of the human hand and the tools it held. So there were rites to bless the magic power of tools. There were other mysteries: of cows and goats and other animals and birds mating – like human beings – and out came life that helped sustain human life. So fertility rites and ceremonies to celebrate life oozing from the earth, or from between the thighs of humans and animals. Human life itself was a mystery: birth, growing up and death, but through many stages. So there were rituals and ceremonies to celebrate and mark birth, circumcision or initiation into the different stages of growth and responsibility, marriages and the burial of the dead.

But see the cruelty of nature: there were droughts and floods, threatening devastation and death. The community shall build wells and walls. But the gods need propitiation. More rituals. More ceremonies. The spirits and the gods were of course invisible but they could be represented by masks worn by humans. Nature, through works and ceremony, could be turned into a friend.

But see the cruelty of human beings. Enemies come to take away a community's wealth in goats and cattle. So there were battles to be fought to claim back one's own. Bless the spears. Bless the warriors. Bless those who defend the community from its enemies without. Victorious warriors returned to ritual and ceremony. In song and dance they acted out the battle scenes for those who were not there and for the warriors to relive the glory, drinking in the communal admiration and gratitude. There were also enemies within: evil doers, thieves, idlers; there were stories – often with a chorus – to point the fate of those threatening the communal good.

Some of the drama could take days, weeks, or months. Among the Agīkūyū of Kenya, for instance, there was the *Ituīka* ceremony held every twenty-five years or so that marked the handing over of power from one generation to another. According to Kenyatta in his book *Facing Mount Kenya*, the Ituīka was celebrated by feasting, dancing and singing over a six-months period. The laws and regulations of the new government were embodied in the words, phrases and rhythmic movements of the new songs and dances.[2] How Ituīka came to be was always re-enacted in a dramatic procession. Central to all these varieties of dramatic expression were songs, dance and occasional mime!

Drama in pre-colonial Kenya was not, then, an isolated event: it was part and parcel of the rhythm of daily and seasonal life of the community. It was an activity among other activities, often drawing its energy from those other activities. It was also entertainment in the sense of involved enjoyment; it was moral instruction; and it was also a strict matter of life and death and communal survival. This drama was not performed in special buildings set aside for the purpose. It could take place anywhere – wherever there was an 'empty space', to borrow the phrase from Peter Brook. 'The empty space', among the people, was part of that tradition.[3]

IV

It was the British colonialism which destroyed that tradition. The missionaries in their proselytising zeal saw many of these traditions as works of the devil. They had to be fought before the bible could hold sway in the hearts of the natives. The colonial administration also collaborated. Any gathering of the natives needed a licence: colonialism feared its own biblical saying that where two or three gathered, God would hear their cry. Why should they allow God above, or the God within the natives to hear the cry of the people? Many of these ceremonies were banned: like the *Ituīka*, in 1925. But the ban reached massive proportions from 1952 to 1962 during the Mau Mau struggle when more than five people were deemed to constitute a public gathering and needed a licence. Both the missionaries and the colonial administration used the school system to destroy the concept of the 'empty space' among the people by trying to capture and confine it in government-supervised urban community halls, schoolhalls, church-buildings, and in actual theatre buildings with the proscenium stage. Between 1952 and 1962 'the empty space' was even confined behind barbed wire in prisons and detention camps where the political detainees and prisoners were encouraged to produce slavishly pro-colonial and anti-Mau Mau propaganda plays.

The social halls encouraged the concert, a kind of playlet, with simple plots often depicting the naive peasant who comes to the big town and is completely perplexed by the complexities of modern life, the stupid peasant who goes to speak to telephone wires asking them to send money to his relatives and leaving the bundle of notes under the telephone pole; and of course the long arm of the law that catches criminals and hence restores peace in the town. The school and church hall produced religious theatre with the story of the prodigal son and the Nativity being among the most popular themes. But the school also produced plays in English; in Alliance High School which I attended Shakespeare, like the *Speech Day*, was an annual event. Between 1955 and 1958 I saw *As You Like It*, *Henry IV Part One*, *King Lear* and *Midsummer Nights Dream* roughly in that order. In the fifties through the British Council and a government-appointed colony-wide drama and music officer, the school drama was systematized into an annual Schools Drama Festival. The many European-controlled theatre buildings erected in the major towns – Mombasa, Nairobi, Nakuru, Kisumu, Kitale, Eldoret – between 1948 and 1952 specialised in West End comedies and sugary musicals with occasional Shakespeare and George Bernard Shaw. The two most famous were the Donovan Maule Theatre in Nairobi, a fully fledged professional theatre and the Kenya National Theatre, a colonial government establishment, projected as a future multi-racial cultural centre. Independence in 1963 did not change the theatre status quo; the 'empty space' was still confined in similar places. West End musicals like *Annie Get Your Gun*, *Boeing Boeing*, *Jesus Christ Superstar*, *Desperate Hours* and *Alice in Wonderland* continued to hold sway, with the expatriate community dominating the professional, the semi-professional and amateur theatre. There was also an Asian language theatre tradition but this was largely confined to Kenyan-Asian community social halls and schools.

The colonial regime also encouraged radio drama with the African as a clown. If the African could be made to laugh at his own stupidity and simplicity he might forget this business of Mau Mau, Freedom, and all that. The drama of the mindless clown was grouped around Kipanga and a few other African comedians.

With independence more and more graduates joined schools and universities and there was a gradual revolt although it was still largely confined to the four walls of the school, the social hall, the university premises, and also to the boundaries of the English language. The revolt of this African petty-bourgeoisie in the area of theatre had roots in the fifties with Alliance High School, Thika, Mang'u, Kagumo and other prominent schools producing a counter-Shakespeare and G. B. Shaw tradition with their own scripts in Kiswahili. At Alliance High School there were *Nakupenda Lakini* by Henry Kuria (who was also organizer of the Kiambu Music Festival) (1954); *Maisha ni Nini* by Kīmani Nyoike (1955); *Nimelogwa nisiwe na mpenzi* by Gerishon Ngūgī (1956); *Atakiwa na Polisi* by B. M. Kurutu (1957) which all ended with performances at Menengai Social Hall in Nakuru, the heartland of settlerdom.

But the revolts of the sixties and the early seventies had a more nationalistic flavour. Kenyan playwrights (like Francis Imbuga, Kenneth Watene, Kibwana and Mīcere Mūgo) and Kenyan directors (like Seth Adagala, Tirus Gathwe, Waigwa Wachiira and David Mulwa) emerged with a growing circle of actors around Voice of Kenya radio and television, the Kenya National Theatre, and the University. Prominent African playwrights and directors from other countries like John Ruganda and Joe de Graft at the University reinforced their Kenyan counterparts. Amateur theatre companies emerged, some flaring only for a day; but a few like 'The University Players' and the Mūmbi wa Maina's 'Tamaduni Players' existed for a longer period. Tamaduni Players were the most consistent in terms of the regularity of their productions, their continuous search for relevance, and their high professionalism.

The revolt took many forms: one was the sheer African petty-bourgeois assertion in the very fact of writing and directing and performing plays. It also took the form of a more and more nationalistic patriotic and anti-neocolonial, anti-imperialist content in the plays, this trend perhaps best exemplified in Mīcere Mūgo's and Ngūgī wa Thiong'o's *The Trial of Dedan Kīmathi* which was performed by the Kenya Festac 77 Drama Group. It also took the form of a more sharpened criticism of the internal order as in Francis Imbuga's *Betrayal in the City* performed by the same group in Nairobi and Lagos.

But the biggest revolt was over the control of the Kenyan National Theatre, set up in the fifties and wholly dominated by British directors and British amateur groups. It remained the preserve of the British expatriate community even after Kenya had her own national anthem and national flag in 1963. It was run by a wholly expatriate governing council with the British Council retaining a representative many years after Independence. There was an outcry over this dominance, from the Kenyan petty-bourgeoisie centred on the University and supported by a few patriotic journalists who called for the Kenyanization of the directorship and council. A statement by the staff of the Literature Department in 1970 denounced the Kenya Cultural Centre as a service station for foreign interests, a statement which was also a cultural reflection of the growing dissatisfaction with the economic and political dominance of imperialist interests in the country as a whole. There was a call for more days and weeks allowed for African theatre. The heated debates climaxed in racial violence in 1976 when one expatriate white lady had her nose bloodied by a black actor after she had called him a black bastard. The police came but in the identification parade she could not make out one African face from another. Seth Adagala, the director of the Kenya Festac 77 Drama Group, and I were later summoned to the C.I.D. headquarters after complaints by the leaders of the European Amateur Groups that we were interfering with the success of their theatrical enterprises, a complaint which was manifestly untrue. But the struggle also took the form of a debate about the whole question, concept and constitution of a National Theatre. Was it just a building? Was it the location? Was it the kind of plays presented there? Or was it simply the skin-colour of the director and the administration staff?

Some groups opted for other premises. The University Theatre, basically an education lecture hall with a stage, wide but not deep, on the same level as the first row of the auditorium, saw a wide range of experimental productions, particularly in the second half of the seventies. Education Theatre II, as it was officially called, became an alternative to the government-owned but foreign-run Kenya National Theatre and Cultural Centre. Tamaduni and other groups staged one innovative play after another under the guidance of the indefatigable Mũmbi wa Maina and other directors.

The running of the Schools Drama Festival, previously in the hands of expatriate staff in the Ministry of Education, now came under the directorship of the first Kenyan African Drama and Literature officer Mr Wasambo Were. Over the years the Festival, which now included a separate but parallel one for the Teachers Training Colleges, had become more and more nationalistic in content as more and more graduates from the University of Nairobi joined the staff of the various schools and brought a new attitude to drama. Under the new officer the Festival took a radical departure from the past. The Festival would move from its annual location at the Kenya National Theatre to a venue in Kakamega, way out in the countryside. Thereafter it would rotate in the provinces with the winning finalist plays touring the country. The language of the plays changed with the English language being edged out by Kiswahili as the main medium of theatrical expression.

The University of Nairobi Literature Department started its own Free Travelling Theatre. The students toured urban and rural community centres and schools to acclaim by thousands. Other travelling mini-theatre groups were formed in other schools and colleges. The accent from the early to mid-seventies was on theatre to the people.

On looking back now, it is clear that Kenyan theatre in the early seventies was trying to break away from the imperialist colonial tradition whose symbols were the European-dominated Kenya National Theatre (albeit aided by the ruling regime), the Donovan Maule Theatre in Nairobi and other similar centres in the major towns.

Its main handicap was still its petty-bourgeois base in the schools and University Colleges, from where came the majority of its actors, directors and plays. Above all it was limited by the very imperialist tradition from which it was trying to break away. English was still accepted as the main medium of revolt and affirmation. Original scripts, even the most radical, were often written from the standpoints of the petty-bourgeoisie. And theatre was still confined within walls. Where it tried to break away from the confines of closed walls and curtains of a formal theatre building into rural and urban community halls, the assumption was still that theatre was to be taken to the people. People were to be given a taste of the treasures of the theatre. People had no traditions of theatre. The assumption that people were to be given theatre was of course in keeping with the government fiction that people were there to be given development particularly if they behaved themselves.

But it was imperialism that had stopped the free development of the national traditions of theatre rooted in the ritual and ceremonial practices of the peasantry. The real language of African theatre could only be found among the people – the peasantry in particular – in their life, history and struggles.

V

Kamĩrĩĩthũ then was not an aberration, but an attempt at reconnection with the broken roots of African civilization and its traditions of theatre. In its very location in a village within the kind of social classes described above, Kamĩrĩĩthũ was the answer to the question of the real substance of a national theatre. Theatre is not a building. People make theatre. Their life is the very stuff of drama. Indeed Kamĩrĩĩthũ reconnected itself to the national tradition of the empty space, of language, of content and of form.

Necessity forced the issue.

For instance, there was an actual empty space at Kamĩrĩĩthũ. The four acres reserved for the Youth Centre had at that time, in 1977, only a falling-apart mud-walled barrack of four rooms which we used for adult literacy. The rest was grass. Nothing more. It was the peasants and workers from the village who built the stage: just a raised semi-circular platform backed by a semi-circular bamboo wall behind which was a small three-roomed house which served as the store and changing room. The stage and the auditorium – fixed long wooden seats arranged like stairs – were almost an extension of each other. It had no roof. It was an open air theatre with large empty spaces surrounding the stage and the auditorium. The flow of actors and people between the auditorium and the stage, and around the stage and the entire auditorium was uninhibited. Behind the auditorium were some tall eucalyptus trees. Birds could watch performances from these or from the top of the outer bamboo fence. And during one performance some actors, unrehearsed, had the idea of climbing up the trees and joining the singing from up there. They were performing not only to those seated before them, but to whoever could now see them and hear them – the entire village of 10,000 people was their audience.

Necessity forced a commonsense solution to the issue of language. Ngũgĩ wa Mĩriĩ and I had been asked to script the initial outline of a play that later came to be called *Ngaahika Ndeenda (I will marry when I want)*. The question was, what language were we going to use?

Since 1960, when as a student I started to scribble words on paper, I had written all my novels and stories in English. Plays too. *The Black Hermit* meant for the celebration of Uganda's Independence was performed by Makerere Students Drama Society at the Uganda National Theatre in 1962. *This Time Tomorrow*, written in 1966, was about the eviction of workers from near the centre of Nairobi to keep the city clean for tourists. In 1976 I had collaborated with Mĩcere Mũgo in writing *The Trial of Dedan Kimathi*. In the preface to the published script we had written what amounted to a literary manifesto calling for a radical change in the attitude of African writers to fight with the people against imperialism and the class enemies of the people. We called for a revolutionary theatre facing the consequent challenge: how to truly depict 'the masses in the only historically correct perspective: positively, heroically and as the true makers of history.' We had gone on to define good theatre as that which was on the side of the people, 'that which, without masking mistakes and weaknesses, gives people courage and urges them to higher resolves in their struggle for total liberation'. But we never asked ourselves how this revolutionary theatre was going to urge people to higher resolves in a foreign language? Indeed in all three plays, *The Black Hermit*, *This Time Tomorrow*, and *The Trial of Dedan Kimathi*, there were very obvious contradictions though these were more apparent on the stage than in the script. In the opening line of *The Black Hermit* the peasant mother is made to speak in a poetic language reminiscent in tone of T. S. Eliot. The elders from a rural outpost come to town for their son, the black hermit, and speak in impeccable English. So does Kĩmaathi, in *The Trial of Dedan Kimathi*, even when addressing his guerrilla army or the peasants and workers in court. Admittedly it is understood that the characters are speaking an African language. But this is only an illusion since they are conceived in English and they speak directly in English. There are other contradictions too: these characters speak English but when it comes to singing they quite happily and naturally fall back into their languages. So they *do* know African languages! The illusion that in speaking English they were really speaking an African language is broken. The realism in theatre collides with the historical reality it is trying to reflect. It is only petty-bourgeois characters – those who have been to schools and universities – who normally and quite freely mix English with African languages in the same sentence or speech.[4]

The use of English as my literary medium of expression, particularly in theatre and the novel, had always disturbed me. In a student's interview in Leeds in 1967 and in my book *Homecoming* (1969) I came back to the question. But I kept on hedging the issue. The possibility of using an African language stayed only in the realm of possibility until I came to Kamīrīīthū.

It was Kamīrīīthū which forced me to turn to Gīkūyū and hence into what for me has amounted to 'an epistemological break' with my past, particularly in the area of theatre. The question of audience settled the problem of language choice; and the language choice settled the question of audience. But our use of Gīkūyū had other consequences in relation to other theatre issues: content for instance; actors, auditioning and rehearsals, performances and reception; theatre as a language.

Ngaahika Ndeenda depicts the proletarisation of the peasantry in a neo-colonial society. Concretely it shows the way the Kīgūūnda family, a poor peasant family, who have to supplement their subsistence on their one and a half acres with the sale of their labour, is finally deprived of even the one-and-a-half acres by a multi-national consortium of Japanese and Euro-American industrialists and bankers aided by the native comprador landlords and businessmen.

The land question is basic to an understanding of Kenya's history and contemporary politics, as indeed it is of twentieth century history wherever people have had their land taken away by conquest, unequal treaties or by the genocide of part of the population. The Mau Mau militant organization which spearheaded the armed struggle for Kenya's independence was officially called the Kenya Land and Freedom Army. The play, *Ngaahika Ndeenda*, in part drew very heavily on the history of the struggle for land and freedom; particularly the year 1952, when the Kīmaathi-led armed struggle started and the British colonial regimes suspended all civil liberties by imposing a state of emergency; and 1963, when KANU under Kenyatta successfully negotiated for the right to fly a national flag, and to sing a national anthem and to call people to vote for a national assembly within every five years. The play showed how that independence, for which thousands of Kenyans died, had been hijacked. In other words, it showed the transition of Kenya from a colony with the British interests being dominant, to a neo-colony with the doors open to wider imperialist interests from Japan to America. But the play also depicted the contemporary social conditions particularly for workers in multi-national factories and plantations.

Now many of the workers and peasants in Kamĩrĩĩthũ had participated in the struggle for land and freedom either in the passive wing or in the active guerrilla wing. Many had been in the forests and the mountains, many in the colonial detention camps and prisons; while some had of course collaborated with the British enemy. Many had seen their houses burnt; their daughters raped by the British; their land taken away; their relatives killed. Indeed Kamĩrĩĩthũ itself was a product of that history of heroic struggle against colonialism and of the subsequent monumental betrayal into neo-colonialism. The play was celebrating that history while showing the unity and continuity of that struggle. Here the choice of language was crucial. There was now no barrier between the content of their history and the linguistic medium of its expression. Because the play was written in a language they could understand the people could participate in all the subsequent discussions on the script. They discussed its content, its language and even the form. The process, particularly for Ngũgĩ wa Mĩriĩ, Kĩmani Gecaũ, and myself was one of continuous learning. Learning of our history. Learning of what obtains in factories. Learning of what goes on in farms and plantations. Learning our language, for the peasants were essentially the guardians of the language through years of use. And learning anew the elements of form of the African Theatre.

What are these elements of form?

First was song and dance. Song and dance as we have seen are central to nearly all the rituals celebrating rain, birth, the second birth, circumcision, marriage, funerals or to all ordinary ceremonies. Even daily speech among peasants is interspersed with song. It can be a line or two, a verse, or a whole song. What's important is that song and dance are not just decorations; they are an integral part of that conversation, that drinking session, that ritual, that ceremony. In *Ngaahika Ndeenda* we too tried to incorporate song and dance, as part of the structure and movement of the actors. The song arises from what has gone before and it leads to what follows. The song and the dance become a continuation of the conversation and of the action. Let me illustrate by quoting a long sequence whose action and movement in time is dependent on a series of songs and dances.

The play opens with Kĩgũũnda and his wife, Wangeci, making preparations to receive Kĩoi and his wife Jezebel. Kĩgũũnda and Wangeci are a peasant family. Kĩoi and Jezebel are a rich landlord family with close connections in high church, banks and industry. Kĩgũũnda works for Kĩoi. But it is the very first time that the Kĩois have visited the Kĩgũũndas and naturally Kĩgũũnda and Wangeci try to puzzle out the reasons for this visit. Why should the landlord want to pay them a visit? Then suddenly it occurs to Wangeci that maybe the Kĩois are coming to discuss the possibilities of a marriage between Gathoni, Kĩgũũnda's daughter, and John Mũhũũni, Kĩoi's son. Mũhũũni has been dating Gathoni. The idea is so farfetched that Kĩgũũnda can only exclaim:

KĨGŨŨNDA:
You women!
You are always thinking of weddings!
WANGECI:
Why not?
These are different times from ours.
These days they sing that love knows no fear.
In any case, can't you see
Your daughter is very beautiful?
She looks exactly the way I used to look – a perfect beauty!
KĨGŨŨNDA: [*stopping dusting up the tyre sandals*]
You? A perfect beauty?
WANGECI:
Yes. Me.
KĨGŨŨNDA:
Don't you know that it was only that
I felt pity for you?
WANGECI:
You, who used to waylay me everywhere all the time?
In the morning,
In the evening,
As I came home from the river,
As I came home from the market,
Or as I came back home from work in the settlers' farms?
Can't you remember how you used to plead with me,
Saying you had never in your life seen a beauty like me?
KĨGŨŨNDA: [*Going back in time*]
That was long before the state of Emergency.
Your heels used to shine bright,

Your face shone like the clear moon at night,
Your eyes like the stars in heaven.
Your teeth, it seemed, were always washed with milk.
Your voice sounded like a precious instrument.
Your breasts were full and pointed like the tip of the sharpest thorn.
As you walked it seemed as if they were whistling beautiful tunes.

WANGECI: [*Also mesmerized by memories of their past youth*]
In those days
We used to dance in Kīneenii forest.

KĪGŪŪNDA:
A dance would cost only twenty-five cents.

WANGECI:
In those days there was not a single girl from Ndeiya up to Gīthīīga
Who did not die to dance with you.

KĪGŪŪNDA:
You too would swing your skirt
Till the guitar player was moved to breaking the strings.
And the guitars used to sound tunes
That silenced the entire forest,
Making even the trees listen . . .

The sound of guitars and other instruments as if KĪGŪŪNDA *and* WANGECI *can hear them in the memory.* KĪGŪŪNDA *and* WANGECI *start dancing. Then they are joined by the guitar players and players of other instruments and* DANCERS. *They dance,* KĪGŪŪNDA *and* WANGECI *among them.*

Nyaangwīcū let's shake the skirt
Nyaangwīcū let's shake the skirt
Sister shake it and make it yield its precious yields.
Sister shake it and make it yield its precious yields.

Nyaangwīcū is danced on one leg
Nyaangwīcū is danced on one leg
The other is merely for pleasing the body.
The other is merely for pleasing the body.

Wangeci the beautiful one
Wangeci the beautiful one
With a body slim and straight like the eucalyptus.

47

With a body slim and straight like the eucalyptus.

Wangeci the little maiden
Wangeci the little maiden
When I see her I am unable to walk.
When I see her I am unable to walk.

Wangeci let's cultivate the fruit garden
Wangeci let's cultivate the fruit garden
This garden that belongs to Kīgūūnda wa Gathoni.
This garden that belongs to Kīgūūnda wa Gathoni.

Wangeci, our mother, we now refuse
Wangeci, our mother, we now refuse
To be slaves in our home,
To be slaves in our home.

When this is over, WANGECI *says, 'Oh my favourite was Mwom-boko.' And* KĪGŪŪNDA *replies: 'Oh in those days we used to tear the right or left side of trouser legs from the knee downwards. Those were our bell bottoms with which we danced Mwomboko.' Now the guitar players and the accordion players start. The Mwomboko* DANCERS *enter.* KĪGŪŪNDA *and* WANGECI *lead them in the Mwomboko dance. Guitars, iron rings and the accordions are played with vigour and the dancers' feet add embellishments.*

The Mwomboko dance is not difficult,
It's just two steps and a turn.
I'll swing you so beautifully that,
Your mother being in the fields,
Your father in a beer feast,
You'll tell me where your father's purse is hidden.
  Take care of me
  I take care of you
  Problems can be settled in jokes.
Limuru is my home
Here I have come to loaf about
Wangeci, my young lady
Be the way you are
And don't add frills
To your present gait.
  Take care of me

I take care of you
Problems can be settled in jokes.
This is your place
Famed for ripe bananas
I'll sing to you till you cry
Or failing to cry
You'll be so overcome with feelings
That you'll take your life.
   Take care of me
   I take care of you
   Problems can be settled in jokes.
I brewed liquor for you
And now you've turned against me!
A cripple often turns against his benefactors
Our son of Gathoni
Good fortune, unexpected, found Wacū in the Field
And she sat down to feast on it.
   Take care of me
   I take care of you
   Problems can be settled in jokes.
Have you taken one too many
Or are you simply drunk
I'll not say anything,
Oh, Wangeci my little fruit,
Until seven years are over . . .

*The voices of men and the sound of guitars, accordions and other
instruments end abruptly. The* DANCERS *leave the stage.* KĪGŪŪNDA
and WANGECI *remain frozen in the act of dancing.* KĪGŪŪNDA *shakes
his head as if he is still engrossed in memories of the past. They
disengage slowly!*

KĪGŪŪNDA:
   Oh, the seven years were not even over
   When we began
   To sing new songs with new voices,
   Songs and voices demanding
   Freedom for Kenya, our motherland.

A procession enters the stage singing freedom songs.

49

Freedom
Freedom
Freedom for Kenya our motherland

A land of limitless joy
A land rich in green fields and forests
Kenya is an African people's country.

We do not mind being jailed
We do not mind being exiled
For we shall never never stop
Agitating for and demanding back our lands
For Kenya is an African people's country . . .

As the SINGERS *leave the stage* WANGECI *takes over the remembrance of things past.*

WANGECI:
  I myself have always remembered
  The Olengarueni women,
  The ones driven from their lands around Nakuru
  To be exiled to Yatta, the land of black rocks.
  They passed through Limuru
  Caged with barbed wire in the backs of several lorries.
  But still they sang songs
  With words that pierced one's heart like a spear.
  The songs were sad, true,
  But the women were completely fearless
  For they had faith and were sure that,
  One day, this soil will be returned to us.

A procession of women SINGERS *enters the stage singing.*

Pray in Truth
Beseech Him with Truth
For he is the same Ngai within us.
One woman died
After being tortured
Because she refused to sell out.

Pray in Truth
Beseech Him with Truth
For he is the same Ngai within us.

Great love I found there
Among women and children
A bean fell to the ground
And it was shared among them.
  Pray in Truth
  Beseech Him with Truth
  For he is the same Ngai within us.

The SINGERS *leave the stage.*

KĪGŪŪNDA:
  It was then
  That the state of Emergency was declared over Kenya.
  Our patriots,
  Men and women of
  Limuru and the whole country,
  Were arrested!
  The Emergency laws became very oppressive.
  Our homes were burnt down.
  We were jailed,
  We were taken to detention camps,
  Some of us were crippled through beatings.
  Others were castrated.
  Our women were raped with bottles.
  Our wives and daughters raped before our eyes!
[*Moved by the bitter memories,* KĪGŪŪNDA *pauses for a few seconds*]
  But through Mau Mau
  Led by Kīmaathi and Matheenge,
  And through the organized unity of the masses
  We beat the whites
  And freedom came . . .
  We raised high our national flag.

A jubilant procession of men, women and children enters the stage singing songs and dances in praise of freedom.

  It is a flag of three colours
  Raise the flag high
  Green is for our earth
  Raise the flag high
  Red is for our blood
  Raise the flag high

51

> *Black is for Africa*
> *Raise the flag high.*

[*They change to a new song and dance*]

SOLOIST:
> *Great our patriots for me . . .*
> *Where did the whites come from?*

CHORUS:
> *Where did the whites come from?*
> *Where did the whites come from?*
> *They came through Mŭrang'a,*
> *And they spent a night at Waiyaki's home,*
> *If you want to know that these foreigners were no good,*
> *Ask yourself:*
> *Where is Waiyaki's grave today?*
> *We must protect our patriots*
> *So they don't meet Waiyaki's fate.*

SOLOIST:
> *Kĩmaathi's patriots are brave*
> *Where did the whites come from?*

[*They continue singing as they walk off the stage.*]

KĨGŨŨNDA:
> How the times run!
> How many years have gone
> Since we got independence?
> Ten and over,
> Quite a good number of years!
> And now look at me!

[KĨGŨŨNDA *looks at himself, points to the title-deed and goes near it*]
> One and a half acres of land in dry plains.
> Our family land was given to homeguards.
> Today I am just a labourer
> On farms owned by Aham Kĩoi wa Kanoru.
> My trousers are pure tatters.
> Look at you.
> See what the years of freedom in poverty
> Have done to you!
> Poverty has hauled down your former splendour.
> Poverty has dug trenches on your face,
> Your heels are now so many cracks,

Your breasts have fallen,
They have nowhere to hold.
Now you look like an old basket
That has lost all shape.

WANGECI:
Away with you,
Haven't you heard it said that
A flower is robbed of the colours by the fruit it bears!
[*Changing the tone of voice*]
Stop this habit of thinking too much about the past
Often losing your sleep over things that had better been
forgotten.
Think about today and tomorrow.
Think about our home.
Poverty has no permanent roots!
Poverty is a sword for sharpening the digging sticks . . .
[*Pauses, as if caught by a new thought*]
Tell me:
What does Kīoi and his family
Want with us today?[5]

As you have seen, the sequence begins with the 'why' of Kīoi's visit,
goes through the entire history of the armed struggle of the fifties
including the achievement of a national flag, and comes back to the
'why' of Kīoi's intended visit. Indeed in *Ngaahika Ndeenda* the past
and the future are often recreated through song and dance and
mime.

Mime in fact is the other most important element of form. The best
example is Kīgūūnda's intended church wedding ceremony. That
sequence starts with Kīgūūnda and Wangeci who are now admiring
their wedding suits and robes having been persuaded to mortgage their
land to a bank to get the means to finance the renewal of their marriage
in church as their African wedding is regarded by the Kīois as sinful
and not valid. They try them on and with mime, music and dance go
through the entire exercise climaxing in their cutting an imaginary five
storied cake.

That mime sequence is also a good illustration of ceremony but one,
in this case, emptied of its grandeur and dignity. The christian
ceremony is externally imposed and lacks the appropriate symbols
rooted in the soil. It becomes a caricature of the national traditions of
ceremony. This is contrasted with the *Ngurario* sequence where,

through the *Gĩtũiro* opera, the dignity of a national ceremony is recreated.

When it came to song, dance and ceremony, the peasants, who of course knew all about it, were particular about the accuracy of detail. Their approach was very serious.

They were also particular about language which, of course, is another element of form. They were concerned that the various characters, depending on age and occupation, be given the appropriate language. 'An old man cannot speak like that' they would say. 'If you want him to have dignity, he has to use this or that kind of proverb.' Levels of language and language-use and the nuances of words and phrases were discussed heatedly.

But what gives any form its tautness and special character and shape is the content. This is even more true in drama. Drama is closer to the dialectics of life than poetry and the fiction. Life is movement arising from the inherent contradiction and unity of opposites. Man and woman meet in a united dance of opposites out of which comes a human life separate from the two that gave it birth but incorporating features of both in such a way that it is recognisable at a glance that so and so is really a product of so and so. The growth of that life depends on some cells dying and others being born. Social life itself arises out of the contradiction between man and nature. But man is part of nature. Karl Marx has said: 'He opposes himself to nature as one of her own forces, setting in motion arms, legs, head and hands, the natural forces of his body, in order to appropriate nature's production to his own wants. By thus acting on the external nature and changing it, he at the same time changes his own nature.'[6] Drama encapsulates within itself this principle of the struggle of opposites which generates movement. There is in drama a movement from apparent harmony, a kind of rest, through conflict to a comic or tragic resolution of that conflict. We end with harmony at a different level, a kind of temporary rest, which of course is the beginning of another movement. The balance of opposing ideas and social forces, of all the contending forces is important in shaping the form of drama and theatre.

The participants were most particular about the representation of history, their history. And they were quick to point out and argue against any incorrect positioning and representation of the various forces – even the enemy forces – at work in the struggle against imperialism. They would compare notes from their own actual experience, whether it was in making guns in the forests, in stealing arms from the British enemy, in carrying bullets through the enemy lines, or in the various strategies for survival. Land and freedom. Economic and political independence. Those were the aims of their struggle and they did not want *Ngaahika Ndeenda* to distort them. The one who made imitation guns for the play at Kamīrīīthū was the very person who used to make actual guns for the Mau Mau guerrillas in the fifties. The workers were keen that the details of the exploitation and the harsh conditions of life in the multinational factories be laid bare. I remember for instance how one group who worked in a particular department at the nearby Bata shoe factory sat down to work out the process and quantity of their exploitation in order to explain it all to those of us who had never worked in a factory. Within a single day they would make shoes to the value of all the monthly wages for the entire work force of three thousand. So they worked for themselves for one day. For whom were they working for the other twenty-nine days? They calculated *what* of *what* they produced went for wear and tear of the machinery and for the repayment of initial capital, and because the company had been there since 1938 they assumed that the initial investment had been repaid a long time ago. To whom did the rest go? To the owners in Canada. What about entrepreneurial skills – the brainpower – which regulated the entire system though seated in offices in Nairobi or far away in Canada? What about the shareholder whose money made the entire system work? Ah, well. They had never seen that brainpower and that shareholder once lift a hammer to make a shoe. If they could make guns and set up armament factories in the harsh conditions of the forest and mountains without the brainpower and money-power of any shareholder from abroad, could they not run a shoemaking factory? The discussion would go on. Thus they were very clear about labour, their labour, being the creator of wealth. But what did that labour get every fortnight or every month? A mere pittance! And what's more, people do die in those factories. Did you know that? People die, people have died. 'Let's count . . . so and so . . .!' I remember one person who as evidence removed his shirt. His body was burned all over. 'Gases', he said. 'And what did I get as compensation? Dismissal. Laid off. Without even a watch for my faithfulness in service.'

The details of the struggle between capital and labour which are described in a long dramatic monologue by one of the worker characters, Gīcaamba, were worked out in discussions. Central to Gīcaamba's monologue explaining to Kīgūūnda that workers are not necessarily better off than the peasants, that the worker and the peasant both suffer from the same system of imperialist capitalism, was the question assumed by the struggle between capital and labour in the twentieth century:

> To have factories and even big industries
> Is good, very good!
> It is a means of developing the country.
> The question is this: who owns the industries?
> Whose children gain from the industries?[7]

The content of the play was asking many questions about the nature of Kenyan society and this generated ever more heated discussions on form and content during the entire period of the play's evolution. Sometimes these involved not just the actual participants but the ever widening circle of the audience.

Auditions and rehearsals for instance were in the open. I must say that this was initially forced on us by the empty space but it was also part of the growing conviction that a democratic participation even in the solution of artistic problems, however slow and chaotic it at times seemed, was producing results of a high artistic order and was forging a communal spirit in a community of artistic workers. PhDs from the university of Nairobi: PhDs from the university of the factory and the plantation: PhDs from Gorki's 'university of the streets' – each person's worth was judged by the scale of each person's contribution to the group effort. The open auditions and the rehearsals with everybody seeing all the elements that went into making a whole had the effect of demystifying the theatrical process.

In the theatre that I was used to in school and colleges and in amateur circles, the actors rehearsed more or less in secrecy and then sprung their finished perfection on an unsuspecting audience who were of course surprised into envious admiration: oh, what perfection, what talent, what inspired gifts – I certainly could never do such a thing! Such a theatre is part of the general bourgeois education system which practises education as a process of weakening people, of making them feel they cannot do this or that – oh, it must take such brains! – In other words education as a means of mystifying knowledge and hence reality. Education, far from giving people the confidence in their ability and capacities to overcome obstacles or to become masters of the laws governing external nature as human beings, tends to make them feel their inadequacies, their weaknesses and their incapacities in the face of reality; and their inability to do anything about the conditions governing their lives. They become more and more alienated from themselves and from their natural and social environment. Education as a process of alienation produces a gallery of active stars and an undifferentiated mass of grateful admirers. The Olympian gods of the Greek mythology or the dashing knights of the middle ages are reborn in the twentieth century as superstar politicians, scientists, sportsmen, actors, the handsome doers or heroes, with the ordinary people watching passively, gratefully, admiringly. Kamīriīthū was the opposite of this. The Kamīriīthū practice was part of education as a process of demystifying knowledge and hence reality. People could see how the actors evolved from the time they could hardly move their legs or say their lines to a time when they could talk and move about the stage as if they were born talking those lines or moving on that stage. Some people in fact were recruited into the acting team after they had intervened to show how such and such a character should be portrayed. The audience applauded them into continuing doing the part. Perfection was thus shown to be a process, a historical social process, but it was admired no less. On the contrary they identified with that perfection even more because it was a product of themselves and their collective contribution. It was a heightening of themselves as a community.

The research on the script of *Ngaahika Ndeenda*, the writing of the outline, the readings and the discussions of the outline, the auditions and rehearsals and the construction of the open-air theatre took in all about nine months – from January to September 1977. The readings, the discussions and the rehearsals were timed to keep in rhythm with the lives of the people. So these were set sometimes on Saturday afternoon but always on Sunday afternoons. Even Sunday afternoon was chosen so that Kamīriīthū theatre would not interfere with church attendance in the mornings.

The results of all this effort to evolve an authentic language of African theatre were obvious when the play opened to a paying audience on 2 October 1977. Once again the performances were timed for Sunday afternoons. Evenings would have been too cold for everybody. *Ngaahika Ndeenda* was an immediate success with people coming from afar, even in hired buses and taxis, to see the show. Theatre became what it had always been: part of a collective festival. Some people knew the lines almost as well as the actors and their joy was in seeing the variations by the actors on different occasions to different audiences. There was an identification with the characters. Some people called themselves by the names of their favourite peasant and worker characters like Kīgūūnda; Gīcaamba; Wangeci; Gathoni.

57

But they also used the names of such characters as *Kīoi, Nditika, Ikuua,* and *Ndugīre,* to refer to those, in and outside the village, who had anti-people tendencies. The language of *Ngaahika Ndeenda* was becoming part of the people's daily vocabulary and frame of reference. There were some touching moments. I remember one Sunday when it rained and people rushed to the nearest shelters under the trees or under the roofs. When it stopped, and all the actors resumed, the auditorium was as full as before. The performance was interrupted about three times on that afternoon but the audience would not go away. The people's identification with Kamīrīthū was now complete.

Later they were driven away, not by the rain, not by any natural disaster, but by the authoritarian measures of an anti-people regime. On 16 November 1977 the Kenya government banned any further public performances of *Ngaahika Ndeenda* by the simple act of withdrawing the licence for any public 'gathering' at the centre. I myself was arrested on 31 December 1977 and spent the whole of 1978 in a maximum security prison, detained without even the doubtful benefit of a trial. They were attempting to stop the emergence of an authentic language of Kenyan theatre.

But that was not the end of Kamīrīthū's search for an authentic language of African theatre in form and content.

In November 1981 they regrouped for another effort, the production of *Maitū Njugīra (Mother sing for me)*. Auditions were set for 7, 14 and 15 November 1981, almost as if Kamīrūthū was resuming the search from the very date and month it had been stopped. I have narrated the fate of this second production in my book, *Barrel of a Pen: Resistance to Repression in Neo-Colonial Kenya.* Here I would like to simply point out that all the elements of theatre developed in 1977 were employed and further extended. *Maitū Njugīra* depicted the heroic struggle of Kenyan workers against the early phase of imperialist capitalist 'primitive' accumulation with confiscation of land, forced labour on the same stolen land and heavy taxation to finance its development into settler run plantations.

Dance, mime, song were more dominant than words in telling this story of repression and resistance. The visual and the sound images carried the burden of the narrative and the analysis. The medium of slides was also introduced to give authentic visual images of the period of the twenties and thirties. And at every stage in its evolution more people from many of the Kenyan nationalities were involved. *Maitū Njugīra (Mother sing for me)*, a drama in music, had more than eighty songs from more than eight nationalities in Kenya all depicting the joy, the sorrow, the gains, the losses, the unity, the divisions, and the march forward as well as the setbacks in Kenyan people's struggles.

Kamīrīīthū was due to put on the musical drama at the Kenya National Theatre on 19 February 1982 after more than ten weeks of strenuous work by what had now become an important alliance from all nationalities of workers, peasants and progressive teachers and students. By going to perform at the Kenya National Theatre the alliance was going to make the point that an authentic language of African theatre, no matter in what specific African tongue it found expression, would communicate to people of all the nationalities. It was also going to prove that this trend had the support of Kenyan people of all the nationalities. Where else to prove this than on the premises of the so-called Kenya National Theatre. It was booked to be the longest run ever even though it was during the off theatre season, at the beginning of the year after Christmas.

The peasants and workers were about to bring national theatre to the capital city. But this was not to be. This time the authorities would not even deign to give a licence, instructions were sent to the management to padlock the doors, and the police were sent to ensure public peace and public security. Our attempts to continue with open rehearsals at the University premises – the famous Theatre II – were again frustrated after about ten such 'rehearsals' seen by about 10,000 people! The University authorities were instructed to padlock the doors of Theatre II. That was on Thursday 25 February 1982. On Thursday 11 March 1982 the government outlawed Kamīrīīthū Community Education and Cultural Centre and banned all theatre activities in the entire area. An 'independent' Kenyan government had followed in the footsteps of its colonial predecessors: it banned all the peasant and worker basis for genuine national traditions in theatre. But this time, the neo-colonial regime overreached itself. On 12 March 1982 three truckloads of armed policemen were sent to Kamīrīīthū Community Education and Cultural Centre and razed the open-air theatre to the ground. By so doing it ensured the immortality of the Kamīrīīthū experiments and search for peasant/worker-based language of African theatre.

A collective theatre, or what Boal has called a 'theatre of the oppressed', was produced by a range of factors: a content with which people could identify carried in a form which they could recognise and identify; their participation in its evolution through the research stages, that is by the collection of raw material like details of work conditions in farms and firms; the collection of old songs and dances like *Mūthīrīgū, Mūcūng'wa,* and *Mwomboko* and opera forms like

59

Gĩtiiro etc; their participation, through discussion on the scripts and therefore on the content and form; through the public auditions and rehearsals; and of course through the performances. The real language of African theatre is to be found in the struggles of the oppressed, for it is out of those struggles that a new Africa is being born. The peasants and workers of Africa are making a tomorrow out of the present of toil and turmoil. The authentic language of African theatre should reflect this even as it is given birth by that very toil and turmoil. Such a theatre will find response in the hearts and lives of the participants; and even in the hearts of those living outside the immediate environment of its physical being and operation.

A 70 year old participant, Njoki wa Njĩkĩra, was interviewed in *The Daily Nation* of Friday 22 January 1982:

> 'When the Kamĩrĩĩthũ Theatre group started', Njoki said, 'we old people found we could be useful by teaching the young some of the things they did not know. I felt I was doing something important to the nation by teaching the songs that we used in *Ngaahika Ndeenda* and that is why I am involved in *Maitũ Njugĩra*' . . . To Njoki the Ngaahika Ndeenda experience showed how history can be brought to the fore through drama so that 'children may know what their past was like and so that they may help in the building of a healthy society. The new play, *Maitũ Njugĩra*, is equally important because very few Kenyans today know what it meant to be colonized in the 1930's which is what the play is about.'[8]

Similar sentiments were expressed by all the others interviewed in the same issue and by others interviewed in *The Standard* of Friday 29 January 1982. Wanjirũ wa Ngigĩ, a young secretary and mother of two summarised it all:

> During rehearsal so far, I have discovered so much I did not know about my own history. I can say with confidence that I know and I'm still learning – a great deal more about my own culture. Knowing more about my past has made me ore sensitive to my present situation and that of my future and the future of my children.[9]

In its short period of physical existence Kamĩrĩĩthũ had an effect on that movement in Kenyan theatre described earlier in this chapter. There was the move towards the people and the gradual but growing confidence in people's languages and their use in theatre. There was also the emergence of people-based cultural festivals like the annual Vihiga Cultural Festival in western Kenya. They were not a copy of

Kamĩrĩĩthũ but were inspired by a similar felt need for a renaissance of Kenyan culture which would be achieved by going to the roots of its being in the lives and languages of the people. The destruction of Kamĩrĩĩthũ was thus much more than a destruction of an open air theatre. In its search for an authentic language of African theatre, Kamĩrĩĩthũ had given palpable form to a vision of Kenya's future – a Kenya for Kenyans, a self-reliant Kenya for a self-reliant people, a vision embodying a communal ethos of democracy and independence. This vision was diametrically opposed to the subservience to the USA and western imperialist interests represented by the neo-colonial regime of both Kenyatta and Moi, which is now embodied in the slogan of Nyayoism which means 'Follow in my footsteps'.

There has been an interesting twist to the Kamĩrĩĩthũ story. In February 1984 President Moi made 'a surprise visit' to Kamĩrĩĩthũ and he shed tears at the poverty he saw around the centre: how can human beings live in such conditions? On 'an impulse', 'an unrehearsed' act of 'personal' generosity, he there and then gave a donation towards the building of a polytechnic where the open air theatre used to be. No mention of the Kamĩrĩĩthũ Community Education and Cultural Centre. But the people were not deceived. A polytechnic was what they were hoping to build. They would welcome one built by the government for after all it was their money. But the regime has different hopes. By its wanton act of destruction of Kamĩrĩĩthũ Theatre in 1982, it had shown its anti-people neo-colonial colours and it had become further alienated from the people. Its intensified repression of Kenyans in 1982 – through detentions without trial or imprisonment on trumped-up charges, particularly of university lecturers and students – did not improve its image and its further alienation from the people. It hopes that people can forget the alternative vision, even though unrealised, but embodied in the Kamĩrĩĩthũ experience. Kamĩrĩĩthũ must not be allowed to become a revolutionary shrine. People have to be taught the virtues of subservience and gratitude to a gallery of stars.

But can an idea be killed? Can you destroy a revolutionary shrine itself enshrined in the revolutionary spirit of a people?

I was in Europe in June 1982 when I heard the news: Dr Kĩmani Gecaũ, chairman of the Literature Department and director of *Ngaahika Ndeenda* in 1977 and co-director, with Waigwa Wachiira, of *Maitũ Njugĩra* in 1981–82, had fled to Zimbabwe. Ngũgĩ wa Mĩrĩĩ, a most dedicated and indefatigable worker for a people's cause, and the coodinating director of Kamĩrĩĩthũ

Community Education and Cultural Centre also had to flee a few hours ahead of those with a warrant for his arrest and possible detention. They have been helping to set up rural-based cultural centres and in 1983 produced *The Trial of Dedan Kimathi* in the Shona language. It was in the same months of June and July 1982 that, as I was about to return to Kenya, I received frantic messages from different directions: orders were out for my arrest and detention without trial on arrival at the Jomo Kenyatta Airport in Nairobi. Should I not delay my return? I did and I have been telling the Kamĩrĩĩthũ story wherever and whenever I have a chance. For on a personal level it has changed my life.

It has led me to prison, yes; it got me banned from teaching at the University of Nairobi, yes; and it has now led me into exile. But as a writer it has also made me confront the whole question of the language of African theatre – which then led me to confront the language of African fiction.

Notes

1 See also Ngũgĩ wa Mĩrĩĩ *On Literary Content* Working paper no. 340, IDS, Nairobi, April 1979. He places his discussion of the literary content at Kamĩrĩĩthũ Community Educational and Cultural Centre in a class analysis of the village community.
2 Jomo Kenyatta *Facing Mount Kenya*, London 1938.
3 I am indebted to Wasambo Were for the comparison between *The Empty Space* of Peter Brook's title, and the practice of African literature during a discussion I had with him on Theatre in Kenya in London 1983.
4 Compare also with Wole Soyinka's *The Lion and the Jewel*, the exchange between Lakunle, the school teacher who quotes abuses from the *Shorter Oxford Dictionary* and Sidi, the illiterate village woman who presumably speaks Yoruba. In what language is Lakunle speaking: Yoruba or English? What about Sidi? In the text they are both speaking English, of course.
5 Ngũgĩ and Ngũgĩ *I Will Marry When I Want*, Nairobi and London 1982, pp. 21–9.
6 Karl Marx *Capital*, Vol. I, Chap. VII, p. 177.
7 Ngũgĩ and Ngũgĩ *I Will Marry When I Want*, Nairobi and London 1982, p. 39.
8 *Daily Nation* 22 January 1982.
9 *The Standard* 29 January 1982. The two features by *The Daily Nation* and *The Standard* carry many other comments and direct quotes from participants which give an insight into the popular base of theatre.

3 *The Language of African Fiction*

I

One of my books *Detained* has the subtitle *A Writer's Prison Diary*. Why a writer's prison diary? Because the main theme was the process of writing a novel under prison conditions. *Caitaani Mũtharabainĩ* (in Engish *Devil on the Cross*) was published by Heinemann in 1980 and it was the first novel of its kind in scope and size in the Gĩkũyũ language.

In discussing the language of African fiction I shall draw heavily on the experience of writing *Caitaani Mũtharabainĩ* and I hope that in the process I shall demonstrate the wider issues and problems of the existence, the origins, the growth and the development of the African novel.

At the time of my arrest at my home on 31 December 1977 I was, in addition to being an active participant in theatre at Kamĩrĩĩthũ Community Educational and Cultural Centre, the Chairman of the Literature Department at the University of Nairobi and Associate Professor. I remember my last lecture. It was to my third year students. 'Next year,' I told them in parting, 'I want to attempt a class analysis of Chinua Achebe's fiction from *Things Fall Apart* up to *Girls at War*. I want in particular to trace the development of the messenger class from its inception as actual messengers, clerks, soldiers, policemen, catechists and road foremen in colonialism as seen in *Things Fall Apart* and *Arrow of God*, to their position as the educated 'been-tos' in *No Longer at Ease*; to their assumption and exercise of power in *A Man of the People*; to their plunging the nation into intra-class civil war in *Girls at War*. And before we meet to discuss all these problems, I urge you to read two books without which I believe it is impossible to understand what informs African writing, particularly novels written by Africans. They are Frantz Fanon's *The Wretched of the Earth*, mostly the chapter titled 'the pitfalls of national consciousness' and V. I. Lenin's *Imperialism, The Highest Stage of Capitalism*.

Five days later – or exactly six weeks after the banning of *Ngaahika Ndeenda* – I was in cell 16 at Kamĩtĩ Maximum Security Prison as a political detainee answering to a mere number K6,77. Cell 16 would become for me what Virginia Woolf had called *A Room of One's Own* and which she claimed was absolutely necessary for a writer. Mine was provided free by the Kenya government.

II

So, confined within the walls of that room of my own, I thought a great deal about my work in the Literature Department – had my students read Frantz Fanon and Lenin on colonialism and imperialism? – and of course about my participation at Kamĩrĩĩthũ Community Educational and Cultural Centre – had the participants continued with adult literacy? – and indeed about my entire situation as a caged writer. The whole point of a neo-colonial regime imprisoning a writer is, in addition to punishing him, to keep him away from the people, to cut off any and every contact and communication between him and the people. In my case the regime wanted to keep me away from the university and the village and if possible to break me. I had to keep my sanity and the best way was to use the very conditions in prison to break that isolation and re-establish a contact despite the bleak walls and the chained doors. My determination became sharpened when a very cruel prison superintendant warned me against any attempts at writing poems – he obviously confused novels with poems.

But why a novel? And why in Gĩkũyũ language?

III

Not so long ago the novel, like God, was declared dead, at least in its eighteenth and nineteenth century forms. There was even a movement in search of a *nouveau roman* but I am not sure whether there was also a parallel movement in search of a new God or, for that matter, whether the search was fruitful. What's clear is that something answering to the name 'novel' has been showing significant signs of life somewhere in Africa and Latin America. The death of the novel was not therefore one of my problems.

Nevertheless the novel, at least in the form that reached us in Africa, is of bourgeois origins. It arose with the emergence of the European bourgeoisie into historical dominance through commerce and industry, with the development of the new technology of the printing press and hence commercial publishing and above all with the new climate of thought that the world was knowable through human experience. At long last the world of Ptolemy was being replaced by the world of Copernicus and Galileo; the world of alchemy by that of chemistry; that of magic and divine wills by that of experience in nature and in human affairs. The Edmunds of the new world were everywhere challenging the King Lears of the old order. A world dominated by nature and its spiritual reflection in God's kingdom both suspiciously possessing all the features of feudal hierarchies of nobles and menials was being replaced by the one dominated by bourgeois man and his spiritual reflection in a God of profit and loss. Today the song is, let labour hold the reins; then the song was, let the bourgeois hold the reins.

The Europe that came to Africa at the end of the nineteenth century had at its head the victorious bourgeois man, now transformed from a captain of industry in a free market system into a commander-in-chief of vast financial resources regulating huge industries and commercial monopolies and in search of new markets to conquer and to govern.

The pre-colonial African world, on the other hand, with different stages of social development among the varied regions and peoples, was on the whole characterised by the low level of development of productive forces. Hence it was dominated by an incomprehensible and unpredictable nature, or rather by a nature to an extent only knowable through ritual, magic and divination. This nature, largely unknowable and largely hostile, could be faced through a collective response and a cohesive social order; it could be cruel in some of its practices, but also humane in its personal relations and its awareness of mutual accountability among its members. This world was reflected in the literature it produced with its mixture of animal characters, of half-man-half-beast and of human beings all intermingling and interacting in a coexistence of mutual suspicion, hostility, and cunning but also occasional moments of co-operation. The social struggles were reflected in another type of literature, that of epic poetic narratives celebrating the heroic deeds of kings and exceptional men who had served the community in times of war or disaster. The internal and external struggles of these societies and hence the development of their productive forces and progressive mastery over nature were hindered by European slavery which often disrupted settled agriculture compelling mass migration and movements.[1] But their natural development was more dramatically hindered and distorted by imperialism. It is true that imperialism – through its heritage of a highly developing science and technology, its amassing of enormous productive forces through a reorganization of the labour of millions under eighteenth and nineteenth century mercantile and industrial capital – brought to Africa the possibilities of knowing and mastering that world of nature. But at the same time it denied the conquered races and peoples the means of knowing and mastering that world. On the contrary their lands were confiscated, their people often killed by a civilisation that had wiped out populations and civilisations in America, New Zealand and Australia. Thus the very means and basis of a progressive ordering of their own lives were taken away from them. The elaborate systems worked out to cope with nature and with one another were often destroyed, leaving human beings at the mercy of a social order more cruel and more incomprehensible in its chaos, its illogicality and its contradictions than nature itself.

For instance the reorganisation of labour under capitalistic agriculture and industry meant productivity and possibilities of wealth on a scale unknown before under feudal and communalistic systems. But the colonial system, through repressive racist ideologies, ensured the private appropriation of that wealth in a few hands, mostly white. Imperialism thus introduced mass poverty and cross regional underdevelopment. Capitalism introduced plenty and possibilities of the conquest of hunger: capitalism ensured poverty and mass starvation on a scale unknown before. Capitalism and the development of science and technology introduced the possibilities of the conquest of nature: capitalism by its uncontrolled use and exploitation of natural resources ensured the virtual dominance of nature over man by way of droughts and desertification. Capitalism introduced a new medical science to conquer diseases: capitalism through its selective prescription of medical care, at least in the colonies, ensured a disease-ridden population who now lacked help from the herbalists and psychiatrists whose practices had been condemned as devilry.

There were other contradictions. Imperialism through the missionaries of its ideology introduced writing to many African languages. It was necessary that the biblical message of subservience, the administrative orders for labour and taxes and the military and police orders for killing recalcitrants, reached the native messengers as directly as possible. Rival imperialisms and the colonial practice of divide and rule introduced contradictory representations of the sound systems of the very same language, let alone of similar African languages within the same colonial boundary. For instance the Gĩkũyũ language had two rival orthographies developed by protestant and catholic missionaries. Before this was rectified, two Gĩkũyũ speaking children could well have been in the position where they could not read each others letters or essays. Again imperialism introduced literacy, but often confined it to clerks, soldiers, policemen, and the petty civil servants, the nascent messenger class about which I was going to talk to my students. Thus even on the eve of independence, the masses of African people could not read or write.

Imperialist nations also introduced the printing press and the possibilities of publishing for a wider audience. For instance in British colonised territories, particularly in East and Central Africa, literature bureaus were established with the commendable and enlightened policy of publishing in English and African languages. But imperialism tried to control the content carried by those languages. Publications were censored directly through government licensing laws or indirectly through the editorial practices of those running the government and missionary presses. African languages were still meant to carry the message of the bible. Even the animal tales derived from orature, which were published by these presses in booklets, were often so carefully selected as to make them carry the moral message and implications revealing the unerring finger of a white God in human affairs.

Thus imperialist pretences to free the African from superstition, ignorance and awe of nature often resulted in deepening his ignorance, increasing his superstitions and multiplying his awe of the new whip-and-gun-wielding master. An African, particularly one who had gone through a colonial school, would more readily relate to the bible with its fantastic explanation of the origins of the universe, its 'divine' revelations about the second coming and its horrifying pictures of hell and damnation for those sinning against imperialist order, than to the novel, with its careful analysis of motive in character and action, and its general assumption that the world in which we live can be understood or at least analysed through observations of patterns of behaviour of individuals or of the changing patterns of human relationships between groups and individuals.

Amidst massive illiteracy, amidst the conflicting phonetic systems even within the same language, amidst the new superstitions of the bible and the church, how can we talk meaningfully of the African novel? How could I contemplate the novel as a means of my reconnection with the people I left behind? My targeted audience – the people – were the two classes represented by Kamīrīīthū. How could I take a form so specifically bourgeois in its origins, authorship and consumption, for such a reconnection with a populace ridden with the problems outlined above?

The social or even national basis of the origins of an important discovery or any invention is not necessarily a determinant of the use to which it can be put by its inheritors. History is replete with examples of the opposite. Gunpowder was invented in China. It was effectively used by the European bourgeoisie in its spread and expansion to all the corners of the globe. Mathematical science was invented by the Arabs but it has been appropriated by all the nations of the earth. The history of science and technology taken as a whole is a result of contributions from many nations and races in Africa, Asia, Europe, America and Australasia. The same is true of the history of the arts – music, dance, sculpture, paintings and literature. African music and art for instance have been appropriated by the Europe and America of the twentieth century. What is true of the national and racial origins of a discovery is even more poignantly true of the class origins of discoveries. The most crucial discoveries and technical breakthroughs that have changed the face of the nineteenth and twentieth centuries like the Spinning Jenny, the weaving loom, and the steam engine were all the products of the working class. All the earlier crucial discoveries like the wheel for irrigation, or the windmill or water-mill, were the inventions of the peasantry. Again this is even more true of the arts. The most important breakthroughs in music, dance and literature have been borrowed from the peasantry. Even the games like football and athletics have come from ordinary people while all the others normally associated with the upper classes were refinements of those of the people. Nowhere is this more clear than in the area of languages. It is the peasantry and the working class who are changing language all the time in pronunciations, in forming new dialects, new words, new phrases and new expressions. In the hands of the peasantry and the working class, language is changing all the time, it is never at a standstill. The social history of the world before the advent of victorious socialism was the continued appropriation of the results and the genius of the labour of millions by the idle classes. Why should not the African peasantry and working class appropriate the novel?

In any case the novel itself was an outgrowth from the earlier traditions of oral tales and of epic poetic narratives like those of Homer's *Iliad* and *Odyssey* or those of Liyongo in Swahili literature. These were certainly the artforms of the peasantry. The African novel as an extended narrative in written form had antecedents in African oral literature. The most essential element in the oral tale as in that of the novel is still the story, the element of what happens next. The artistry lies in the various devices for maintaining the story.

Perhaps the crucial question is not that of the racial, national, and class origins of the novel, but that of its development and the uses to which it is continually being put.

IV

The African novel and its development, since its inception early this century, have been adversely affected by two factors.

The printing press, the publishing houses and the educational context of the novel's birth were controlled by the missionaries and the colonial administration. The early practitioners of the African novel, particularly in South Africa, were products of missionary educational institutions and they were more likely to have been exposed to Bunyan's *Pilgrim's Progress* and the King James or Authorized version of the bible than to Tolstoy, Balzac or Dickens. Even when later novels were introduced in the school libraries, the selection was carefully done so as not to expose the young minds to dangerous, undesirable and unacceptable moral and political influences. I remember one day at Alliance High School, the missionary headmaster using the morning assembly to lecture us on the beauty and the dignity of Alan Paton's novel *Cry the Beloved Country* in which a subservient non-violent African christian Uncle Tom is the hero; and then later he accused Alan Paton of going astray in the next novel, *Too late the Phalarope*, by introducing sex sequences between whites and blacks in South Africa. The early African novel produced under such circumstances, took its themes and moral preoccupation from the bible. But such a novel was also the product of a deliberate policy of the government and mission-controlled presses. In Rhodesia the Literature Bureau would not publish an African novel which had any but religious themes and sociological themes which were free from politics. Retelling old fables and tales, yes. Reconstructions of precolonial magical and ritual practices, yes. Stories of characters who move from the darkness of the pre-colonial past to the light of the christian present, yes. But any discussion of or any sign of dissatisfaction with colonialism. No!

The second adverse factor was the rise of universities and colleges on the African soil at the beginning of the fifties. (A parallel movement was the education of the same type of student in universities abroad.) Makerere University College in Uganda, Ibadan University College in Nigeria and the Ghana University College were all overseas colleges of the University of London. They had fully-fledged departments of English: for the first time there was growing up a group of African students who were being exposed to more than the King James Bible and Bunyan's *Pilgrim's Progress*. They had studied the English novel from Richardson to James Joyce. They would also be familiar with, or at least be aware of, the American, the French and the Russian novel. They would also read European novelists like Joseph Conrad and Joyce Cary or Alan Paton, some of whose books had Africa as their thematic subject. Many of these English departments also founded literary journals or student magazines like *Horn* in Ibadan and *Penpoint* in Makerere. But these students turned to English as the vehicle of their fictional encounter with their Africa. The brilliant minds of a Chinua Achebe, a Wole Soyinka or a Kofi Awoonor went not to revitalise the African novel but to create a new tradition, that of the Afro-European novel. The novel (in English, French or Portuguese) found further encouragement through the multinational publishers who saw a new literary area for investment. The Afro-European novel is now almost inseparable from Heinemann's African Writers Series with more than a hundred novels on its list. But publishers like Longman and homegrown varieties like the East African Publishing House also have impressive lists.

Thus the African novel was further impoverished by the very means of its possible liberation: exposure of its would-be-practitioners to the secular tradition of the critical and socialist realism of the European novel and the entry on the stage of commercial publishers who were outside the colonial government and missionary control.

I was part and parcel of that process, or rather one of its products. I went to Makerere University College in 1959 and read English. My earliest short story, 'Mūgumo' was first published in the department magazine, *Penpoint*, under the title, 'The Fig Tree'. By 1969 I had completed my first novel manuscript which later became *The River Between*. By 1963 *Weep Not, Child*, my second novel manuscript, had been accepted by William Heinemann, London and it later became the seventh title in the African Writers Series. 1977, the year of my arrest and political detention, had seen the publication of my fourth novel in English, *Petals of Blood*.

It was natural that, as I sat in Cell 16 at Kamiti Maximum Security Prison in 1978, I should have been thinking of the novel as the means of my defiance of the intended detention of my mind and imagination. Under the prison circumstances the novel had other advantages. Theatre and film, the ideal means for breaking through the barriers of illiteracy, involve more than one person and indeed a fixed location or premises, not to mention financial investment in the case of film. The novel, at least the writing of it, needs only *pen* and *paper*. Nevertheless, I had first to resolve the question of language which was clearly inseparable from the question of to which tradition I would reconnect myself: that of the Afro-European Novel to which *A Grain of Wheat* and *Petals of Blood* belonged or that of the African novel of which I had no previous experience. No neutrality. I had to choose.

But in a sense the choice had been settled for me by Kamīrīīthū and by the very fact of my detention. I would attempt a novel in the very language which had been the basis of incarceration. I would reconnect myself not to the Afro-European novel of my previous practice but to the African novel of my new commitment.

V

The road to that decision had been long. As I have explained I grew up speaking Gīkūyū. My first encounter with stories and oral narratives was through Gīkūyū. As a new literate in Gīkūyū, I avidly read the bible, particularly the stories in the Old Testament. I also read most of the booklets then available in Gīkūyū language and published mostly by the missionary and government presses; for example *Moohero Ma Tene*, *Mwendo Nī Ira na Irūri*, *Kariūki na Mūthoni* or *Mūikarīre ya Aagīkūyū* were not novelettes or creative stories as such but thinly fictionalised descriptions of old customs, traditions, stages in the life of a Mūūgīkūyū child or straight biblical narrative. They were full of moral lessons derived from the bible or from the old traditions. The most creative of those Kenyans then writing in Gīkūyū was Gakaara wa Wanjaū who had even established his own Gakaara Book Service for publishing and book distribution. He had an impressive list of novelettes, political essays, songs and poems and sheer agitational material, all urging people to higher resolves in their pursuit of land, freedom and the redemption of their culture. Unfortunately all his books were banned and he himself arrested and detained for ten years from 1952 to 1962. But his books, like *Riūa Rītaanathūa, O Kĩrĩma Ngaagũa, Mageria Nomo Mahota, Ngwenda Ũũnjũrage* and *Marebeta Ikũmi ma wendo* remained tantalising titles in my mind. I thereafter drifted to what was then available in Kiswahili. Again not much. But I read and re-read *Hekaya Za Abunuwasi*, being the stories and adventures of a trickster, Abunuwasi.

The English language opened the door to a wide range of fiction and it was this that eventually led me to the English Department at Makerere in 1959 and hence to the kind of writing which climaxed in *Petals of Blood* which was published in July 1977. But I was becoming increasingly uneasy about the English language. After I had written *A Grain of Wheat* I underwent a crisis. I knew whom I was writing about but whom was I writing for? The peasants whose struggles fed the novel would never read it. In an interview in 1967 with *Union News*, a student newspaper in Leeds University, I said: 'I have reached a point of crisis. I don't know whether it is worth any longer writing in English.' The Obi Wali challenge of 1963 kept on pursuing me through Leeds and after. In June 1969 while based at Makerere University as a Fellow in Creative Writing in the Department of English, I wrote a paper 'Towards a National Culture' as part of the background material for the 1969 Unesco Conference on 'Cultural Policy in Africa' held in Dakar, Senegal. The paper was later included in my book *Homecoming* and in it I was more emphatic about the language issue:

> Equally important for our cultural renaissance is the teaching and study of African languages. We have already seen what any colonial system does: impose its tongue on the subject races, and then downgrade the vernacular tongues of the people. By so doing they make the acquisition of their tongue a status symbol; anyone who learns it begins to despise the peasant majority and their barbaric tongues. By acquiring the thought-processes and values of his adopted tongue, he becomes alienated from the values of his mother tongue, or from the language of the masses. Language after all is a carrier of values fashioned by a people over a period of time. It seems to me that in a country where ninety per cent speak African languages, it is very unwise not to teach these in schools and colleges. We need to develop a national language, but not at the dire expense of the

regional languages. In a socialist economic and political context, the development of ethnic languages would not be inimical to national unity and consciousness. It is only in a competitive capitalist set-up that the warring interests exploit ethnic and regional language differences to the detriment of the common cause of the peasantry and the workers. That a study of our own languages is important for a meaningful self-image is increasingly being realized . . .

. . . Increased study of African languages will inevitably make more Africans want to write in their mother tongues and thus open new avenues for our creative imagination.[2]

In 1977 the Kamĩrĩĩthũ experience led me to give a public lecture at Kenyatta University College in which I called upon Kenyan writers to return to their roots in the languages and cultures of all our nationalities.

Still the question nagged me. I had been able to cope with the problem of language in theatre. What about a novel? Would I be able to overcome the problems? Kamĩtĩ Maximum Security Prison finally resolved the issue. In a challenge to the imprisoning authorities through *The Detainees Review Tribunal* and dated 23 June 1978 I concluded:

Kenyan writers have no alternative but to return to the roots, return to the sources of their being in the rhythms of life and speech and languages of the Kenyan masses if they are to rise to the great challenge of recreating, in their poems, plays and novels, the epic grandeur of that history.

Instead of being suppressed and being sent to maximum security prisons and detention camps, they should be accorded all the encouragement to write a literature that will be the pride of Kenya and the envy of the world.[3]

But by then I was already in the middle of my first novel in Gĩkũyũ language or rather I should say that I was deep in the problems of writing *Caitaani Mũtharabainĩ*, in prison, in Cell 16.

VI

Paper and pen were the first problem. One could get a pen if one said that one was writing an appeal or a confession to the authorities.

One could even get two or three sheets or paper. But a whole pile for a novel? I resorted to toilet paper. Whenever I have said this people have laughed or looked at me with questions in their eyes. But there was no mystery to writing on toilet paper. Toilet paper at Kamĩtĩ was meant to punish prisoners. So it was very coarse. But what was bad for the body was good for the pen.

But there were other problems that had nothing to do with the fact that the room of one's own was Cell 16. Words for instance. Sentences. Paragraphs. In *Four Quartets* T. S. Eliot has made the apt observation on the slippery quality of words:

> Words strain,
> Crack and sometimes break, under the burden,
> Under the tension, slip, slide, perish,
> Decay with imprecision, will not stay in place,
> Will not stay still.

I found this even more true while writing *Caitaani Mũtharabainĩ*. Gĩkũyũ language did not have a significant tradition of novel or fiction writing. Gakaara wa Wanjaũ had tried to create the beginnings of such a tradition. But his books had been banned in the fifties. After independence he established a journal in the Gĩkũyũ language called *Gĩkũyũ Na Mũmbi*. He ran a fictional series on the adventures of *Kĩwaĩ wa Nduua*. But it did not have the quality of his writings in the fifties which were still mostly out of print. I was also confronted with basic questions of tense, even those of the changing visual impression of words on paper. Words and tenses were even more slippery because of the unsatisfactory Gĩkũyũ orthography. Gĩkũyũ language had been reduced to writing by non-native speakers such as European missionaries and they could not always identify the various lengths of vowels. The distinction between the short and the long vowel is very important in Gĩkũyũ prose and poetry. But the prevailing orthography often left the reader to guess whether to prolong or shorten the vowel sound. This would be very tiring for an extended piece of prose. This lack of the means of making distinction between the long and short vowel sound assumed a previous knowledge of all the words on the part of the reader. I tried to solve the problem by using double vowels where I wanted to indicate the long vowel. But it took several pages before I could get used to it. And even then it was never finally satisfactory for what it called for was a new letter or a new marker for the long vowel. Gĩkũyũ is also a tonal language but the prevailing orthography did not indicate tonal variations.

So for all these reasons, I would write a paragraph in the evening sure of how it read, only later to find that it could be read in a different way which completely altered the meaning. I could only solve the problem by severely controlling the context of words in a sentence, and that of sentences in a paragraph, and that of the paragraph within the entire situation of the occurrence of the action in time and space. Yes, words did slip and slide under my own eyes. They would not stay in place. They would not stay still. And this was often a matter of great frustration.

But the biggest problem then, and what I still think is the biggest problem facing the growth and the development of the African novel, is finding the appropriate 'fiction language', that is with fiction itself taken as a form of language, with which to effectively communicate with one's targeted audience: that is, in my case, the people I left behind.

There were two interrelated problems of 'fiction language' vis-à-vis a writer's chosen audience: his relationship to the form, to the genre itself; and his relationship to his material, that is to the reality before him. How would he handle the form? How would he handle the material before him?

The first question has to do with how the novel as a form has developed. Defoe is different from George Eliot, certainly from Balzac, Zola, Tolstoy and Dostoevsky. What about Joseph Conrad, James Joyce, and Faulkner with their handling of points of view, time, character and plot? The Afro-European novel itself had produced a whole range of approaches: from the linear plot development in Chinua Achebe's *Things Fall Apart* to Wole Soyinka's *The Interpreters* which almost dispenses with plot. Could I write for an audience that had never read a novel in the same way as I would write for an audience that had read or was aware of James Joyce, Joseph Conrad, Wole Soyinka or Ayi Kwei Armah?

In the Afro-European novel of my previous practice I had gone through different phases of 'technical' growth. *The River Between* and *Weep Not, Child* have a linear plot. One action leads to the next along the normal sequence and divisions of time – seconds, minutes, hours, days, weeks, months, years. Event leads to event in a relay in a field of continuous time. It is the biographical approach where the character/narrator follows the hero in time and space from his/her point of entry to that of exit, let's say from birth to death. The point of view is largely that of the central character. The one narrative voice is that of the omniscient narrator/author. But by the time *Weep Not, Child* came

75

out in 1964 I was already dissatisfied with that approach. In the works of Joseph Conrad, which I had studied as a special paper, I had seen how the author had used a variety of narrative voices at different times and places in the same novel with tantalising effect. With Conrad the same event could be looked at by the same person at different times and places; and each of these multiple voices could shed new light on the event by supplying more information, more evidence, or by relating other episodes that preceded or followed the event under spotlight. *Nostromo* was my favourite. I still think it is a great novel, but on the whole I found Conrad's vision limited. His ambivalence towards imperialism – and it was imperialism that supplied him with the setting and subject matter of his novels – could never let him go beyond the balancing acts of liberal humanism. But the shifting points of view in time and space; the multiplicity of narrative voices; the narrative-within-a-narration; the delayed information that helps the revision of a previous judgement so that only at the end with the full assemblage of evidence, information and points of view, can the reader make full judgement – these techniques had impressed me.

George Lamming had also impressed me in his masterly handling of different narrative techniques within the same novel, particularly in *In the Castle of My Skin*. The omniscient narrator; drama; the diary; reportage; autobiography; third person narration and direct authorial intervention to take the side of a character; all these are used by Lamming in varying ways in his early novels *In the Castle of My Skin*, *The Emigrants*, *Of Age and Innocence*, and *Season of Adventure*. Lamming's anti-imperialist consistency, his commitment to third world struggles, his clear base in peasant and worker, and the social political issues in his work, brought his world close to me and my experience of life in Kenya.

My further acquaintance with Gogol, Dostoevsky, Tolstoy, Gorky, Sholokov, Balzac and Faulkner had shown me more possibilities for the novel in terms of thematic concerns and range of technique.

Now my own observation of how people ordinarily narrated events to one another had also shown me that they quite happily accepted interventions, digressions, narrative within a narrative and dramatic illustrations without losing the main narrative thread. The story-within-a-story was part and parcel of the conversational norms of the peasantry. The linear/biographical unfolding of a story was more removed from actual social practice than the narrative of Conrad and Lamming.

The narrative form of *A Grain of Wheat* with its stories within stories in a series of flashbacks was a product of that reappraisal. The multiple narrative voices, apart from helping me in coping with flexible time and space, also helped me in moving away from a single character novel. In *A Grain of Wheat* all the main characters are of almost equal importance, and the people – the village people – in their motion in history are the real hero of the novel. The present action of the novel takes place within four days before independence day in 1963. But within that there is constant movement in time and space from the present to the beginning of the century and to other intermediate periods. *Petals of Blood* had taken a stage further the techniques of flashbacks, multiple narrative voices, movement in time and space and parallel biographies and stories. The technique allowed me to move freely in time and space through the centuries and through all the important landmarks in Kenya's history from the early times and back to the twelve days duration of the present of the novel.

But all this assumed a reader acquainted with the convention of reading novels, and particularly the modern novel in European languages. Would similar techniques carry the kind of reader who had been to see *Ngaahika Ndeenda* (*I will marry when I want*) at Kamĩrĩĩthũ? And yet how would I return to the linear plot? I was, in other words, much more conscious of my new audience. Or maybe it was a matter of languages. Would my use of Gĩkũyũ language dictate a different kind of novel?

Whatever the case, I wanted to go for a simpler plot, a simpler or clearer narrative line, a stronger story element (the element of what happens next!) without looking down upon or patronising the intended worker/peasant readership.

I tried to solve the problem in three ways. I went for a fairly simple structure, that of a simple journey. *Caitaani Mũtharabainĩ* (*Devil on the Cross*) rests on two main journeys over virtually the same ground. Warĩĩnga moves in a matatũ taxi from the capital city Nairobi to Ilmorog, a fictional rural outpost. Then Warĩĩnga makes a second journey in a car from Nairobi to Ilmorog to Nakuru. A gap of two years separates the two journeys. There are a number of flashbacks. But they are all controlled by the time and space progression on the two layers of parallel journeys that suggest other journeys. The journey, the means of transport and the actual places mentioned in Nairobi and Nakuru would be familiar to many ordinary Kenyans. I also borrowed heavily from forms of oral narrative, particularly the conversational tone, the fable, proverbs, songs and the whole tradition of poetic self-praise or praise of others. I also incorporated a biblical element – the parable – because many literates would have read the bible. People would be familiar with these features and I hoped that these would help root the novel within a known tradition.

Language; plot; realism of social and physical detail; features of oral narratives: all these were elements of form and I knew that form by itself, no matter how familiar and interesting, could never hold the attention of my new kind of reader for long. They have more important things to do than indulge in pretty rearrangements of familiar features of orature or of the urban and rural landscape. Content with which the people could identify or which would force them to take sides was necessary. Content is ultimately the arbiter of form. A proper marriage of content and form would decide the reception accorded the novel. So the most important thing was to go for a subject matter, for a content, which had the weight and the complexity and the challenge of their everyday struggles.

And this brought me to the next problem: my relationship to my material, that is to the historical reality of a neo-colony.

A writer's handling of reality is affected by his basic philosophic outlook on nature and society and his method of investigating that nature and society: whether for instance he perceives and therefore looks at a phenomenon in its interconnection or in its dislocation; in its rest or in its motion; in its mutability or immutability; in its being or in its becoming; and whether he sees any qualitative change in its motion from one state of being into another. A writer's handling of the material can also be affected by his material base in society, that is his class position and standpoint. This, I hasten to add, does not necessarily produce good or bad writing, or rather a consciously held outlook does not necessarily make for bad or good writing for this ultimately depends on that undefinable quality of imagination, a writer's artistry, which is able to perceive what is universal – that is, applicable to the widest possible scale in time and space – in its minutest particularity as a felt experience. But it does affect his approximation of reality or rather his effectiveness in correctly reflecting reality.

But what happens when reality is stranger than fiction? How does a novelist capture and hold the interest of the reader when the reality confronting the reader is stranger and more captivating than fiction? And yet this is what confronts a novelist in a neo-colony vis-à-vis the audience most adversely affected by that very reality of a neo-colony.

Let me give a few concrete examples from recent history.

VII

July 1984: the President of the West German Federal Council, Franz Josef Strauss, makes an official visit to the independent republic of Togo in West Africa, at the invitation of President Eyadema. The occasion? To denounce the Berlin conference of 1884? To draw lessons from it to guide the relations between Western Europe and Africa into a new footing of complete economic, political and cultural equality? Oh no. This occasion is to celebrate the one hundredth anniversary of the unequal treaty imposed on King Mlapa III of Togo to establish the kingdom as a colony of the German Reich. President Eyadema even erects a statue of the German Imperial Eagle (or is it American?) to commemorate not the resistance to colonisation but the glory of colonisation. The Governor-General's residence is rebuilt. And all this is to be paid for by Togolese peasants and workers. And so 1884, which is always remembered by millions of African people as the year of historic shame, the start of a century of continuous humiliation of Africa by the West, is being celebrated with pride by an African President. A West German newspaper columnist (see *Nordbayerischer Kurier* 6 July 1984) goes straight to the point: 'it can be assumed that in Togo Strauss and his hosts will move on the same wavelength. And so it should be. Here we Germans need not feel a guilty conscience because the time of our colonial rule was too short to leave behind traces other than nostalgic ones.'[4] Right. The time of the more recent German attempts at the colonisation of the other European nations was even shorter. Does that maybe leave even greater traces of nostalgia in the 'we Germans' of the Markus Cleven's July commentary? The fault is not really the West German journalist's. After all there were no West German gunships at the coast to force this grovelling act of collective self-abnegation on the Togolese Presidency. Only the Mark (aid) to help extract more Marks (profits) from the Togolese people. And President Eyadema is waiting for his share or commission.

There are other absurdities. Mobuto of Zaire, in an act of supreme African authenticity, has ceded a whole territory many times the size of New Zealand to a West German rocket company. A group of African leaders recently begged France to send troops to Chad to protect French legitimate interests, threatened by 'imperialist' Libya, Moi of Kenya has given military bases to U.S.A. without a debate in parliament, with Kenyans only later learning about the 'secret' deal through a debate in U.S. Congress. One could quote other even more incredible episodes, of the callous massacre of children, of the equally callous genocide of part of a population and all by native leaders on behalf of imperialism. For the point is this: the Mobutus, the Mois and the Eyademas of the neo-colonial world are not being forced to capitulate to imperialism at the point of an American maxim gun. They themselves are of the same mind: they are actually begging for a recolonisation of their own countries with themselves as the neo-colonial governors living in modern fortresses. They are happier as the neo-slave drivers of their own peoples; happier as the neo-overseers of the U.S.-led economic haemorrhage of their own countries.

How does a writer, a novelist, shock his readers by telling them that these are neo-slaves when they themselves, the neo-slaves, are openly announcing the fact on the rooftops? How do you shock your readers by pointing out that these are mass murderers, looters, robbers, thieves, when they, the perpetrators of these anti-people crimes, are not even attempting to hide the fact? When in some cases they are actually and proudly celebrating their massacre of children, and the theft and robbery of the nation? How do you satirise their utterances and claims when their own words beat all fictional exaggerations?[5]

As I contemplated the neo-colonial reality of Kenya I was confronted with the question of the fictional form of its depiction. But a writer, any writer, has only one recourse: himself, those images that often flit across the mind, those mental reflections of the world around. The chemistry of imagination transforms the quantity of these different images, reflections, thoughts, pictures, sounds, feelings, sights, tastes, all the sense impressions, into a coalescence of a qualitatively different but unified image or sets of images of reality.

In search of the image that would capture the reality of a neo-colony that was Kenya under both Kenyatta and Moi, I once again fell on the oral tradition.

VIII

For a long time I had been intrigued by the Faust theme in literature. The theme reappears in several works of European literature: Marlowe's *Faustus*, Goethe's *Faust*, Thomas Mann's *Dr Faustus* and Bulgakov's *Master and Margarita*. But I always suspected that the story of the good man who surrenders his soul to evil for immediate earthly gains of wealth, intellect and power was universal and was rooted in the lores of the peasantry. Elements of it are to be found in many national traditions. Owuor Anyumba, a colleague in the Department of Literature who had done immense work on the oral literature of the different nationalities in Kenya, had told me instances of this in a number of stories involving sorcerers. Once in 1976 travelling to western Kenya with Kavetsa Adagala, another colleague in the Department, I saw for the first time the human shaped rocks of Idakho. I had this strange sensation of suddenly coming across something I had been looking for and in returning to Limuru, I wrote more than a hundred pages of a novel. The working title? *Devil on the Cross* but in English. My work at Kamīrīīthū in 1977 made me lose all interest in the novel. In prison I tried to remember the story but I could not recall a single incident of what I had written. But those Idakho rocks remained in my mind. What legends about those human shaped rocks had the peasants built? The images of Idakho fused with images of those maneating ogres in Gīkūyū orature. Marimū were supposed to possess two mouths, one in front and the other at the back. The one at the back was covered with long hair. They were cruel, very greedy, and they lived on the labour of humans. What about the latter day Marimūs? Would the Marimū characters provide me with the image I sought?

In my reading of the work of the South Korean poet Kim Chi Ha I had seen, particularly in the *Five Bandits* and *Groundless Rumours*, how effectively he had exploited the oral forms and images to confront the South Korean neo-colonial realities. Satire is certainly one of the most effective weapons in oral traditions.

And then one day I got it. Why not tell the story of men who had sold their souls and that of the nation to the foreign devil of imperialism? Why not tell the story of evil that takes pride in evil? Why not tell the story of robbers who take pride in robbing the masses?

That was how I came to write the novel *Caitaani Mūtharabainī* in Gīkūyū language. *Caitaani Mūtharabainī (Devil on the Cross)* tells the story of Warīinga and six others who travel in a matatū taxi from Nairobi to Ilmorog. The passengers find that they have something in common. They all have invitations to a feast of thieves and robbers organized by the devil. At the heart of the feast is a competition to choose the seven cleverest thieves and robbers – that is those who have developed the art of robbing the people to the highest degree. The competitors have to stand in front of the others to tell their exploits and achievements. For instance there is the case of one robber who has become so wealthy through smuggling that he begins to resent his wealth. Why? Because though he has got all that quantity of money, he has one heart and one life like all the other humans including his victims. But the breakthrough in heart transplants gives him an idea. He has visions of a huge factory for manufacturing spare parts of the human body including extra penises so that a really rich man could buy immortality and leave death as the prerogative of the poor. But he makes a mistake in telling his wife about the vision. She is delighted at the possibility of the wives of the rich being distinguished from the wives of the poor by their two mouths, two bellies, two or more hearts and two cunts:

'When I heard her mention two female organs and say that she would be able to have two instead of one, I was horrified. I told her quite frankly that I would not mind her having two mouths, or two bellies, or multiples of any other organ of the body. But to have two . . . no, no! *I told her to forget all that nonsense.* Then she started arguing, and said that if that was to be the case, then I wasn't going to be allowed two cocks. I asked her bitterly: 'Why do you want to have two? Tell me: what would you use two for?' She retorted: 'Why do you want two? What would you use two for? If you have two, then I must have two. *We must have equality of the sexes.'*

'By this time, I was really very angry! I told her to take *equalities* to Europe or America. *Here we are Africans*, and we must *practise African culture*. I struck her a blow on the face. She started crying. I struck her again. But just as I was about to strike her a third time, she surrendered. She said I could have three, or ten. She would be satisfied with just one.

'People, think about that vision! Every rich man could have two mouths, two bellies, two cocks, two hearts – and hence two lives! Our money would buy us immortality! We would leave death to the poor! Ha! ha! ha!

'Bring me the crown. At long last, it has found its rightful owner!'

IX

The reception of a given work of art is part of the work itself; or rather, the reception (or consumption!) of the work completes the whole creative process involving that particular artistic object. So now I want to tell you briefly how the novel, *Caitaani Mūtharabainī* was received. It was read in families. A family would get together every evening and one of their literate members would read it for them. Workers would also gather in groups, particularly during the lunchbreak, and they would get one of them to read the book. It was read in buses; it was read in taxis; it was read in public bars.

One amusing aspect of all this was the development of 'professional readers' – but in bars. These were people who would read the book aloud to the other drinking but attentive customers. When the reader reached an interesting episode and he discovered that his glass was empty, he would put the book down. 'Give him another bottle of beer!' some of the listeners would shout to the proprietor. So our reader would resume and go on until his glass was empty. He would put the book down and the whole drama would be repeated, night after night, until the end of the novel.

The process I'm describing is really the appropriation of the novel into the oral tradition. *Caitaani Mūtharabainī* (*Devil on the Cross*) was received into the age old tradition of storytelling around the fireside; and the tradition of group reception of art than enhances the aesthetic pleasure and provokes interpretation, comments and discussions. Remnants of this – what used to be the norm, that is the group reception of art – are still to be found in theatre and, to a limited extent, in the cinema.

The distribution of the novel (and of the play *Ngaahika Ndeenda* which was published at the same time) was a challenge to the publishers. It soon became clear that the structure of bookshops, libraries and other information centres was geared to serve the urban English-educated sectors. The urban poor and the rural areas had really no access to luxuries in between hard covers. They are presumed to be illiterate – which they normally are – and poor – which they mostly are. How does one overcome the isolation imposed by poverty and illiteracy? Do these not severely limit the reception of, let's say, a novel? All this is probably true: poverty and illiteracy do severely limit access to knowledge and information. This is a structural problem and goes to the economic and political basis of accessibility of knowledge, information, literature. But after some time institutions are built around this uneven and unequal development. The lack of bookshops and library facilities in the rural areas where the majority live is a case in point. They are poor and illiterate; therefore they cannot buy or read books; therefore there is no need for bookshops or libraries. But because no bookshops or libraries are available, people are denied the very means of knowledge and information which might help in their attempt to organise and break the circle of illiteracy. Rural schools are denied what is freely available to the wealthy sections of the urban centres. The habit of borrowing a book from a library or buying a book for reading for pleasure and for instruction outside the formal classroom is hardly developed. How do you sell novels to such areas? There was no real solution to the problem. The publishers often used their vans as a mobile bookshop. They experimented in various ways: like leaving several copies at some shops or stalls on a sale or return basis. But some enthusiastic readers would buy the books from the publishers in bulks of five, ten or twenty and on their own initiative would take the copies to rural areas and plantations. There were some surprises. One such seller, Ngigĩ wa Wachiira, on returning to a plantation where a month before he had sold two or three copies, was greeted with gifts. So out there there were such good books. Would he please keep on bringing new titles to them? They could always pool their resources and buy a few copies, and so Ngigĩ had become a hero for making *Caitaani Mũtharabainĩ*, a novel, available to them!

Despite the difficulties, the novel sold fairly well – certainly to the commercial satisfaction of the 'daring' publisher. The publishers had initially printed only 5,000 copies, hoping to sell them over a period of three to five years. In other words they would have been satisfied with an annual sale of over a thousand copies. But within a month of publication they had reprinted another 5,000 and within the same year they had to reprint 5,000 more. The novel came out in April 1980. By December 1980, they had had three printings bringing the total to 15,000 copies. Not even for a novel in English had they ever done so well in Kenya in the same length of time. The publishers tell me now the novel has settled to an annual sale of about 1000 copies which compares favourably with their best-selling titles in English or Kiswahili in Kenya.

The novel has now been translated into English, Swedish, Norwegian and German. There are possibilities of Russian and Japanese editions. But more important has been the translation of the novel into Kiswahili under the title *Shetani Msalabani*, a direct communication between Gĩkũyũ and Swahili languages.

Indeed I see this kind of communication between African languages as forming the real foundation of a genuinely African novel. A novel originally written in Ibo could find itself translated into Yoruba and vice versa. A novel written in Dholuo or Maasai could find itself translated into two or three or more Kenyan languages or into African languages outside Kenya. There would thus be a real dialogue between the literatures, languages and cultures of the different nationalities within any one country – forming the foundations of a truly national literature and culture, a truly national sensibility! Within Africa as a whole there would be the foundation of a truly African sensibility in the written arts. This will also have the added effect of enhancing the art of translation which would be studied in schools and colleges (another career open to graduates!) and this necessarily would mean more rigorous and committed study of African languages. Each thing will be feeding on every other thing, in a dialectical sense, to create a progressive movement in the African novel and literature.

X

The future of the African novel is then dependent on a willing writer (ready to invest time and talent in African languages); a willing translator (ready to invest time and talent in the art of translating from one African language into another); a willing publisher (ready to invest time and money) or a progressive state which would overhaul the current neo-colonial linguistic policies and tackle the national question in a democratic manner; and finally, and most important, a willing and widening readership. But of all these other factors, it is only the writer who is best placed to break through the vicious circle and create fiction in African languages. The writer of fiction can be and must be the pathfinder. It has happened in history, in other countries such as Russia and Finland. Then the other factors will follow. When that day comes, when the African writer will naturally turn to African languages for his creative imagination, the African novel will truly come into its own, incorporating into itself all the features developed in the different parts of Africa from the different cultures of African peoples as well as the best progressive features of the novel or fiction developed in Asia, Latin America, Europe, America, the World.

It is therefore too early to make any conclusion about the character of the language of the African fiction and particularly the African novel. And here I am also talking of fiction as a language. But I am convinced that it will find its form and character through its reconnection with the mainstream of the struggles of African people against imperialism and its rooting itself in the rich oral traditions of the peasantry. In doing this it will play a most crucial role in Africa's general quest for relevance.

Notes

1 'No human disaster, with the exception of the Flood (if that biblical legend is true) can equal in dimension of destructiveness the cataclysm that shook Africa. We are all familiar with the slave trade and the traumatic effect of this on the transplanted black but few of us realize what horrors were wrought on Africa itself. Vast populations were uprooted and displaced, whole generations disappeared, European diseases descended like the plague, decimating both cattle and people, cities and towns were abandoned, family networks disintegrated, kingdoms crumbled, the threads of cultural and historical continuity were so savagely torn asunder that henceforward one would have to think of two Africas: the one *before* and the one *after* the Holocaust.' Ivan Van Sertima, New Brunswick and London 1984, p. 8.

2 Ngũgĩ wa Thiong'o *Homecoming*, London 1972, pp. 16–17.

3 Ngũgĩ wa Thiong'o *Detained: A Writer's Prison Diary*, London 1981, p. 196.

4 Markus Cleven *Nordbayerischer Kurier* 6 July 1984.

5 The philosophy of President Moi of Kenya is called 'Nvayoism', i.e. follow my footsteps. Recently he has elaborated on that philosophy in words that beat the most inventive satiric genius when he demanded that all Kenyans must sing like parrots:

> 'Ladies and Gentlemen, we Kenyans are happy apart from the fact that there is widespread drought. I would like to say, while here with you, that for progress to be realised there should be no debates in newspapers on this and that. What is required is for people to work in a proper manner . . .
>
> '. . . I call on all ministers, assistant ministers and every other person to sing like parrots. During Mzee Kenyatta's period I persistently sang the Kenyatta (tune) until people said: This fellow has nothing (to say) except to sing for Kenyatta. I say: I didn't have ideas of my own. Why was I to have my own ideas? I was in Kenyatta's shoes and therefore, I had to sing whatever Kenyatta wanted. If I had sung another song, do you think Kenyatta would have left me alone? Therefore you ought to sing the song I sing. If I put a full stop, you should also put a full stop. This is how this country will move forward. The day you become a big person, you will have the liberty to sing your own song and everybody will sing it . . .' An excerpt from President Moi's speech on his return from Addis Ababa on 13 September 1984

What beats all satiric descriptions is that some University academics, some journalists, and of course most of the MPs and ministers have actually been echoing Moi's every word – like parrots. They have nothing to say for their colleagues under false charges or detention without trial, but are voluble about anybody described by the neo-colonial regime as being a 'dissident'.

4 *The Quest for Relevance*

I

So far I have talked about language in creative literature generally and in theatre and fiction in particular. I should have gone on to talk about 'The language of African poetry' but the same arguments apply even more poignantly in the area of poetry. The existence and the continuing growth of poetry in African languages, clearly and unequivocally so in orature (oral literature), make it manifestly absurd to talk of African poetry in English, French or Portuguese. Afro-European poetry, yes; but not to be confused with African poetry which is the poetry composed by Africans in African languages. For instance, written poetry in Swahili goes back to many centuries. While the poetic political compositions of the great anti-imperialist Somali fighter, Hassan, will be known by heart by every Somali-speaking herdsman, not a line by even the best of African poets in foreign languages will be known by any peasant anywhere in Africa. As for a discussion of the other language of poetry – where poetry, like theatre and fiction, is considered as a language in itself with its own structures of beats, metres, rhymes, half-rhymes, internal rhymes, lines and images – it calls for different resources including a knowledge of the particular African languages of its expression, which I cannot, at present, even pretend to possess.

Instead, I shall attempt to sum up what we have so far been discussing by looking at what immediately underlies the politics of language in African literature; that is the search for a liberating perspective within which to see ourselves clearly in relationship to ourselves and to other selves in the universe. I shall call this 'a quest for relevance' and I want to look at it as far as it relates, not to just the writing of literature, but to the teaching of that literature in schools and universities and to the critical approaches. In other words, given that there is literature in Africa and in the world, in what order should it be presented to the child and how? This involves two processes: the choice of material and the attitude to, or interpretation of, that material. These two processes will themselves affect and be affected by the national and the class bases of the choice and the attitude to the material chosen. Finally the national and even the class bases of our choice and perspective will affect and be affected by the philosophic base from which we look at reality, a matter over which there can never be any legislation. Already as you can see we are entangled in a kind of vicious circle with everything affecting and being affected by everything else. But let me explain the question of base.

How we see a thing – even with our eyes – is very much dependent on where we stand in relationship to it. For instance we are all in this lecture theatre. But what we see of the room and how much of it we see is dependent on where we are now sitting as we listen to this talk. For instance you all can see the wall behind me: and I can see the wall behind you. Some of you are seated in such places as physically allow you to see much more of this room than others. What is clear is that were we to leave this room and describe it, we would end up with as many descriptions of this room as there are people here tonight. Do you know the story of the seven blind men who went to see an elephant? They used to have so many conflicting speculations as to the physical make-up of an elephant. Now at last they had a chance to touch and feel it. But each touched a different part of the animal: leg, ear, tusk, tail, side, trunk, belly and so they went home even more divided as to the physical nature, shape and size of an elephant. They obviously stood in different positions or physical bases in their exploration of the elephant. Now, the base need not be physical but could also be philosophical, class or national.

In this book I have pointed out that how we view ourselves, our environment even, is very much dependent on where we stand in relationship to imperialism in its colonial and neo-colonial stages; that if we are to do anything about our individual and collective being today, then we have to coldly and consciously look at what imperialism has been doing to us and to our view of ourselves in the universe. Certainly the quest for relevance and for a correct perspective can only be understood and be meaningfully resolved within the context of the general struggle against imperialism.

It is not always easy to see this in literature. But precisely because of that, I want to use the example of the struggle over what is to be taught, and in what order, with what attitudes or critical approaches, to illustrate the anti-imperialist context of the quest for relevance in

Africa today. I want to start with a brief description of what has been called 'the great Nairobi literature debate' on the teaching of literature in universities and schools.

II

The debate started innocuously when on 20 September 1968 the then head of the English Department, Dr James Stewart, presented proposals to the Arts Faculty Board on the development of the English Department. The proposals were in many ways pertinent. But they were all preceded by two crucial sentences:

> The English department has had a long history at this college and has built up a strong syllabus which *by its study of the historic continuity of a single culture throughout the period of emergence of the modern west* makes it an important companion to History and to Philosophy and Religious Studies. However, it is bound to become less *British*, more open to other writing in English (American, Caribbean, African, Commonwealth) and also to continental writing, for comparative purposes.[1]

A month later on 24 October 1968 three African lecturers and researchers at the University responded to Dr Stewart's proposals by calling for the abolition of the English Department as then constituted. They questioned the underlying assumption that the English tradition and the emergence of the modern west were the central root of Kenya's and Africa's consciousness and cultural heritage. They rejected the underlying notion that Africa was an extension of the West. Then followed the crucial rejoinder:

> Here then, is our main question: if there is a need for a 'study of the historic continuity of a single culture', why can't this be African? Why can't African literature be at the centre so that we can view other cultures in relationship to it?[2]

Hell was let loose. For the rest of 1968 and spilling over into 1969 the debate raged on, engulfing the entire faculty and the university. Thus within four sentences the stage was set for what has become the most crucial debate on the politics of literature and culture even in Kenya of today. What was interesting was that the details of the debate were the same: all sides were agreed on the need to include African,

European and other literatures. But what would be the centre? And what would be the periphery, so to speak? How would the centre relate to the periphery? Thus the question of the base of the take-off, the whole question of perspective and relevance, altered the weight and relationship of the various parts and details to each other.

In order to see the significance of the debate and why it raised so much temper we have to put it in a historical context of the rise of English studies in Africa, of the kind of literature an African student was likely to encounter and of the role of culture in the imperialist domination of Africa.

III

English studies in schools and higher institutions of learning became systematised after the Second World War with the setting up of the overseas extensions of the University of London in Uganda, Nigeria, Ghana, Sierra Leone, Kenya and Tanzania; and with very few variations they offered what also obtained in London. The syllabus of the English Department for instance meant a study of the history of English literature from Shakespeare, Spencer and Milton to James Joyce and T. S. Eliot, I. A. Richards and the inevitable F. R. Leavis. Matthew Arnold's quest for the sweetness and light of a hellenized English middle class; T. S. Eliot's high culture of an Anglo-Catholic feudal tradition, suspiciously close to the culture of the 'high table' and to the racial doctrines of those born to rule; the Leavisite selected 'Great Tradition of English Literature' and his insistence on the moral significance of literature; these great three dominated our daily essays. How many seminars we spent on detecting this moral significance in every paragraph, in every word, even in Shakespeare's commas and fullstops? For some reason the two most outstanding critical minds that might have made my study of English Literature really meaningful even in a colonial setting – Arnold Kettle and Raymond Williams – were studied, if at all, only remotely and fleetingly even in the time from 1959 to 1964. But here I am not looking at which writer or critic was more suitable to our situation or even the difference in their world outlook. What was more important was that they all fell within English tradition except in the study of drama where names like those of Aeschylus, Sophocles and Aristotle or Ibsen, Chekhov, Strindberg and Synge would appear quaint and strange in their very unEnglishness. The centrality and the universality of the English tradition was summed up in the title of an inaugural lecture by Professor Warner of Makerere, *Shakespeare in Africa*, in which he grew almost ecstatic about the fact that some of his students had been able to recognise some characters of Jane Austen's novels in their own African villages. So, English literature was applicable to Africa too: the defence of English studies in an African situation was now complete. In schools the English language and English literature syllabuses were tailored to prepare the lucky few for an English degree at university. So the syllabuses had the same pattern. Shakespeare, Milton, Wordsworth, Shelley, Keats and Kipling were familiar names long before I knew I would even make it to Makerere.

In my book, *Writers in Politics* – particularly in the essay 'Literature and Society' – I have tried to sum up the kind of literature available to African children in the classrooms and libraries for their school and university education, by placing it into three broad categories.

First was the great humanist and democratic tradition of European literature: Aeschylus, Sophocles, Shakespeare, Balzac, Dickens, Dostoevsky, Tolstoy, Gorky and Brecht to mention just a few names. But their literature, even at its most humane and universal, necessarily reflected the European experience of history. The world of its setting and the world it evoked would be more familiar to a child brought up in the same landscape than to one brought up outside, no matter how the latter might try to see Jane Austen's characters in the gossiping women of his rural African setting. This was not helped by a critical tradition that often presented these writers, Shakespeare included, as if they were mindless geniuses whose only consistent quality was a sense of compassion. These writers, who had the sharpest and most penetrating observations on the European bourgeois culture, were often taught as if their only concern was with the universal themes of love, fear, birth and death. Sometimes their greatness was presented as one more English gift to the world alongside the bible and the needle. William Shakespeare and Jesus Christ had brought light to darkest Africa. There was a teacher in our school who used to say that Shakespeare and Jesus used very simple English, until someone pointed out that Jesus spoke Hebrew. The 'Great Tradition' of English literature was the great tradition of 'literature'!

Then there was the literature of liberal Europeans who often had Africa as the subject of their imaginative explorations. The best example is Alan Paton's *Cry the Beloved Country*. Here an African eschewing violence, despite the racist violence around him, is the perfect hero. The Reverend Stephen Kumalo is presented in such a way that all our sympathies are with him. He is the embodiment of the biblical man who offers the enemy the left cheek to strike, after the right cheek has already been bashed in by the same enemy. Kumalo is the earlier literary version in an African setting of those Americans in the sixties who thought they could stop the Vietnam war by blowing bubbles and offering flowers to club and gun wielding policemen. Joyce Cary in *Mister Johnson* had gone a stage further in his liberalism. In this novel he offered an idiotic African as the hero. Mister Johnson is the dancing, fun-loving African full of emotional vitality and the endearing human warmth of a child. In the novel he is condemned to death. What was his dearest wish? To be shot dead by the European District Officer. The District Officer grants him that wish. Don't we do the same for our horses and cats? The point is that in the novel the reader is supposed to admire both the District Officer and Mister Johnson: they have established a human contact – that of the rider and the horse, the master and his servant. Karen Blixen's book *Out of Africa* falls within the same liberal mould: to her Africans are a special species of human beings endowed with a great spirituality and a mystical apprehension of reality or else with the instinct and vitality of animals, qualities which 'we in Europe' have lost.

The third category was the downright racist literature of writers like Rider Haggard, Elspeth Huxley, Robert Ruark, and Nicholas Monsarrat. In such a literature there were only two types of Africans: the good and the bad. The good African was the one who co-operated with the European coloniser; particularly the African who helped the European coloniser in the occupation and subjugation of his own people and country. Such a character was portrayed as possessing qualities of strength, intelligence and beauty. But it was the strength and the intelligence and the beauty of a sell-out. The bad African character was the one who offered resistance to the foreign conquest and occupation of his country. Such a character was portrayed as being ugly, weak, cowardly and scheming. The reader's sympathies are guided in such a way as to make him identify with Africans collaborating with colonialism and to make him distance himself from those offering political and military resistance to colonialism. One can see the same schema at work today in the portrayal of the various African regimes in the Western media. Those regimes, as in Kenya and Ivory Coast, which have virtually mortgaged the future of their countries to Euro-American imperialism, are portrayed as being pragmatic, realistic, stable, democratic and they are often shown as having achieved unparalleled economic growth for their countries. But other regimes like those of Nkrumah's Ghana or Nasser's Egypt which strove for a measure of national self-reliance are portrayed as being simplistic, unrealistic, doctrinaire, authoritarian and are often shown as having brought only economic chaos to their countries. Thus imaginative literature had created the necessary racist vocabulary and symbols long before the T.V. and the popular media had come to dominate the scene.

African children who encountered literature in colonial schools and universities were thus experiencing the world as defined and reflected in the European experience of history. Their entire way of looking at the world, even the world of the immediate environment, was Eurocentric. Europe was the centre of the universe. The earth moved around the European intellectual scholarly axis. The images children encountered in literature were reinforced by their study of geography and history, and science and technology where Europe was, once again, the centre. This in turn fitted well with the cultural imperatives of British imperialism. In this book I have in fact tried to show how the economic control of the African people was effected through politics and culture. Economic and political control of a people can never be complete without cultural control, and here literary scholarly practice, irrespective of any individual interpretation and handling of the practice, fitted well the aim and the logic of the system as a whole. After all, the universities and colleges set up in the colonies after the war were meant to produce a native elite which would later help prop up the Empire. The cool, level-headed servant of the Empire celebrated in Kipling's poem 'If'; the gentleman who could keep his head against the rising storms of resistance; the gentleman who would meet with triumph and disaster and treat those two imposters just the same; the gentleman who had not the slightest doubt about the rightness of colonialism despite the chorus of doubt around; this gentleman was now being given African robes in the post-war schools and universities of an ageing imperialism.

The structures of the literary studies evolved in the colonial schools and universities had continued well into independence era completely unaffected by any winds of cultural change. The irony of all this was that these departments were being run in countries where the oral tradition, the basis of all genres of written literature be it a poem, a play, or a story, was beating with life and energy, and yet they were unaffected by the surging creative storm all around them. The study of the historic continuity of a single culture throughout the period of emergence of the modern west was still the organising principle of literature teaching in schools and colleges.

Seen against this background, the rejection of that principle in 1968 was therefore more than a rejection of a principle in a literary academic debate. It was questioning the underlying assumptions behind the entire system that we had inherited and had continued to run without basic questions about national perspective and relevance. The question is this: from what base do we look at the world?

IV

Three lecturers, Owuor Anyumba, Taban Lo Liyong and myself, were emphatic in our rejection and affirmation: our statement said,

> We reject the primacy of English literature and cultures. The aim, in short, should be to orientate ourselves towards placing Kenya, East Africa and then Africa in the centre. All other things are to be considered in their relevance to our situation and their contribution towards understanding ourselves . . . In suggesting this we are not rejecting other streams, especially the western stream. We are only clearly mapping out the directions and perspectives the study of culture and literature will inevitably take in an African university.[3]

We proposed a new organising principle which would mean a study of Kenyan and East African literature, African literature, third world literature and literature from the rest of the world. We concluded:

> We want to establish the centrality of Africa in the department. This, we have argued, is justifiable on various grounds, the most important one being that education is a means of knowledge about ourselves. Therefore, after we have examined ourselves, we radiate outwards and discover peoples and worlds around us. With Africa at the centre of things, not existing as an appendix or a satellite of other countries and literatures, things must be seen from the African perspective.[4]

But our boldest call was for the placing, within the national perspective, of oral literature (orature) at the centre of the syllabus:

> The oral tradition is rich and many-sided . . . the art did not end yesterday; it is a living tradition . . . familiarity with oral literature could suggest new structures and techniques; and could foster

attitudes of mind characterized by the willingness to experiment with new forms . . . The study of the Oral Tradition would therefore supplement (not replace) courses in Modern African Literature. By discovering and proclaiming loyalty to indigenous values, the new literature would on the one hand be set in the stream of history to which it belongs and so be better appreciated; and on the other be better able to embrace and assimilate other thoughts without losing its roots.[5]

Orature has its roots in the lives of the peasantry. It is primarily their compositions, their songs, their art, which forms the basis of the national and resistance culture during the colonial and neo-colonial times. We three lecturers were therefore calling for the centrality of peasant and worker heritage in the study of literature and culture.

The new organising principle was accepted after a long debate which engulfed the entire University and which, at one time, also included all the participants at the 1969 Nairobi Conference of English and Literature Departments of the Universities of East and Central Africa. African Orature; literature by Africans from the Continent, the Caribbean, and Afro-America; literature of 'third' world peoples from Asia and Latin America; literature from the rest of the world including Europe and North America; roughly in that order of relevance, relationship and perspective, would form the basis of a new literature syllabus with English as the mediating language. The actual syllabus resulting from the 1968–9 debate was necessarily a compromise. For instance East African poetry was to be taught in *its European context*. It was not until 1973, when the majority of the staff in the department were Africans, that the syllabus was streamlined to reflect the new perspectives without a qualifying apologia.

The growth of the Literature Department at the University of Nairobi, a department which has produced students who can, by starting from their environment, freely link the rural and urban experiences of Kenyan and African literature to that of Garcia Marquez, Richard Wright, George Lamming, Balzac, Dickens, Shake-speare and Brecht is a far cry from those days in the fifties and sixties when they used to try and detect Jane Austen's characters in their villages.

V

But that was not the end of the Nairobi Literature Debate.[6] In September 1974 a crucial conference on 'The Teaching of African Literature in Kenyan Schools' was held at Nairobi School. The conference was jointly organised by the Department of Literature, University of Nairobi and the Inspectorate of English in the Ministry of Education. It was attended by two hundred secondary school teachers of literature and English; the staff of the departments of literature and of the faculties of education, University of Nairobi and Kenyatta University College; delegates from departments of literatures of Dar es Salaam, Makerere and Malawi Universities; representatives of the Inspectorate of English, Ministry of Education and of the Kenya Institute of Education; observers from the Ministry of Education in Tanzania and Uganda; representatives from the then East African Community; East Africa Examination Council; East Africa Literature Bureau; trade union delegates from the Kenya National Union of Teachers (KNUT); and four publishers: Jomo Kenyatta Foundation, East African Literature Bureau, East Africa Publishing House and Oxford University Press. As if to give it an even more truly international character, there were visiting delegates from the University of West Indies at Mona, Jamaica, the University of Ife, Nigeria and from Auckland University, New Zealand. This impressive gathering was the result of hard organisational efforts of the steering committee chaired by Eddah Gachukia and S. A. Akivaga.

The conference was clearly motivated by the same quest for relevance which earlier had led to the reconstitution of the Department of Literature. In the recommendations of a working committee elected by the conference, it is argued that:

> Prior to independence, education in Kenya was an instrument of colonial policy designed to educate the people of Kenya into acceptance of their role as the colonized. The education system at independence was therefore an inheritance of colonialism so that literature syllabuses were centred on the study of an English literary tradition taught by English teachers. Such a situation meant that Kenyan children were alienated from their own experience [and] identity in an independent African country.[7]

Addressing itself to questions of language and literature, a resolution passed at the end of the conference stated:

The present language and literature syllabuses are inadequate and irrelevant to the needs of the country. They are so organised that a Kenyan child knows himself through London and New York. Both should therefore be completely overhauled at all levels of our education system and particularly in schools.[8]

The conference, which was charged with examining the role of literature in society and the nature of literature taught in secondary schools and its relevance to Kenya's present day needs, called for the centrality of oral literature as a take-off base to comtemporary literature. They argued that a sound educational policy was one which enabled students to study the culture and the environment of their society first, then set it in relation to the culture and environment of other societies: 'African literature, literature of the African diaspora, and all other literatures of related experiences must be at the core of the syllabuses.'[9] A working committee set up by the conference with Dougal Blackburn as Chairman and R. Gacheche as the Secretary came up with detailed recommendations on policy and on syllabuses along the principles outlined in the conference resolution. The seventy-three page document was titled: *Teaching of Literature in Kenya Secondary Schools – Recommendations of the Working Committee* and was clearly the result of months of hard work and commitment.

Looking at the document ten years later, one is struck, not so much by their critique of the existing syllabuses or by their detailed proposals for change – though both are impressive and still relevant to the similar debates and issues today – but by the consciousness that guided the critique and the proposals.

The pan-African consciousness is strong. The authors see Africa as one and they reject the division of Africa into sub-saharan (Black Africa; Real Africa) and Northern (Arabic; Foreign; Mediterranean Africa). They want a Kenyan child to be exposed to the literature from north, south, west and east Africa:

The centuries old Arab civilization has exerted tremendous in-fluence on the literature of modern North Africa and also many parts of the continent. To date their influence has been denied by our educators and the literature of North Africa and the Arab world has largely been ignored.[10]

The authors want to pursue the African connection to the four corners of the earth, so to speak, and they want Kenyan children to be exposed to those historical links of biology, culture and struggle, particularly in Afro-American and Caribbean literature:

It is often asked, why study Caribbean and Afro-American literature? What is the connection between African and the West Indian and Afro-American?

(a) We have the same bio-geographic roots: the people of the West Indies and Afro-America are Africans who, a few hundred years ago, were brutally uprooted from the African continent.

(b) We have shared the same past of humiliation and exploitation under slavery, and colonialism: we have also shared the glorious past of struggle, and fight against the same force.

(c) Equally important we have the same aspirations for the total liberation of all the black people, in the world.

Their literature, like our literature embodies all the above aspects of *our struggle for a cultural identity*.

Apart from that, African peoples of the Diaspora have contributed much to Africa's cultural and political growth. Blyden, C. L. R. James, George Padmore, W. E. Dubois, Marcus Garvey and many others were part and parcel of Africa's struggle for independence. The literary movements from the West Indies and from Afro-America have creatively interacted with those in Africa. Aimé Césaire, Frantz Fanon, Claude McKay, Langston Hughes, Léon Damas, René Dépestre, Paul Robeson – all these giants of culture and the arts have positively contributed to the growth of African Literature.

Most of these comments would apply equally well to the literature of the third world especially that of Asia and Latin America.[11]

Africa; African connections; third world; indeed, the authors of the report are very conscious of the internationalist setting and context of the national experience. Like the university Literature Department, which was conscious of the immense value of world literature, they too refused to substitute national chauvinism for the British colonial chauvinism of the existing syllabuses. A Kenyan child would be exposed to world literature and the democratic tradition in world literature.

In accordance with the principle of teaching beginning with the students' immediate environment and moving out towards the world, the teaching of non-African literature in schools should aim to introduce the Kenyan student to *the world context of the black experience*. Such study should therefore include European and American literature, with their historical and present influences on the societies and literatures of black peoples, and a study of literature from other parts of the third world such as Latin America and Asia. Criteria for selection should attempt to balance: literary excellence, social relevance, and narrative interest. *The aim is to instil in the student a critical love of literature, which will both encourage its pursuit in later years and ensure that such a pursuit is engaged in fruitfully* . . . Given the nature of Kenyan society, we recommend that attention be paid to literature expressing the experience of a changing society, and that it be ensured that the variety of experience of different classes in society be covered.[12]

Their recommendations for the teaching of world literature come face to face with the issue of language; and they have authors which include Tolstoy, Gogol, Gorky, Dostoevsky (Russian); Zola, Balzac, Flaubert (French); Ibsen (Norwegian); Faulkner, Arthur Miller, Upton Sinclair, Hemingway (American); Dickens, Shakespeare, Conrad, Yeats, Synge (British and Irish); Mann and Brecht (German). They see the necessity or inevitability of continued use of English, but they strongly call for Swahili to be made compulsory in all schools but particularly for those students of English and literature and drama:

A clear programme of Swahili literature be introduced and be made compulsory in schools.

Every language has its own social and cultural basis, and these are instrumental in the formation of mental processes and value judgements. Whereas it is accepted that we use English and will continue to do so for a long time to come, the strength and depth of our cultural grounding will ultimately depend on our ability to invoke the idiom of African Culture in a language that is closer to it. Swahili has a major and an increasing role to play in Kenya, and needs to be given greater emphasis than it has hitherto been accorded.

An immediate step that should be taken to fulfill this aim is that adequate numbers of Swahili teachers should be trained.[13]

All in all, the report is shot through and through with a consciousness that literature is a powerful instrument in evolving the cultural ethos of a people. They see literature as part of the whole ideological mechanism for integrating a people into the values of a dominant class, race, or nation. Imperialism, particularly during colonialism, provides the best example of how literature as an element of culture was used in the domination of Africa. The report notes:

> That Africa as a continent has been a victim of forces of colonial exploitation, oppression and human degradation. In the field of culture she was taught to look on Europe as her teacher and the centre of man's civilization, and herself as the pupil. In this event Western culture became the centre of Africa's process of learning, and Africa was relegated to the background. Africa uncritically imbibed values that were alien and had no immediate relevance to her people. Thus was the richness of Africa's cultural heritage degraded, and her people labelled as primitive and savage. The colonizer's values were placed in the limelight, and in the process, evolved a new African who denied his original image, and exhibited a considerable lack of confidence in his creative potential.[14]

The writers are therefore shocked that syllabuses designed to meet the needs of colonialism should continue well into the independence era.

> It was noted with shock and concern that even ten years after Independence, in practically every school in the republic our students were still being *subjected to alien cultural values which are meaningless especially to our present needs.* Almost all books used in our schools are written by foreign authors; out of 57 texts of drama studied at EAACE level in our schools between 1968 and 1972 only one was African. It became obvious that very little is being done in schools to expose our students to their cultural and physical environment.[15]

They are therefore conscious of the fact that an actual literature syllabus, no matter how far reaching in its scope and composition of texts and authors, is limited unless literature is seen and taught as an ideological component of the continuing national liberation process. In one of their conclusions they write:

> Three major principles that emerged from the conference have guided the discussions of the working committee and the preparation of this final report.
>
> (i) *A people's culture is an essential component in defining and revealing their world outlook. Through it, mental processes can be conditioned, as was the case with the formal education provided by the colonial governments in Africa.*
>
> (ii) A sound educational policy is one which enables students to *study the culture and environment of their own society first, then* in relation to the culture and environment of other societies.

(iii) *For the education offered today to be positive and to have creative potential for Kenya's future it must be seen as an essential part of the continuing national liberation process.*[16]

The hell let loose by the conference and by its subsequent recommendations was almost a repeat of the 1968–9 University-based debate. But now the debate became national. Some newspapers opened their pages to the literature debate revealing in the process a wide range of views on the issue from extreme hostility to passionate commitment. Believe it or not, in the early seventies academics and teachers could hold such a debate and assert the primacy of the Kenyan people and their experience of the history of struggle without fear of being labelled Marxist, Communist or radical and being hauled into prisons and detention camps. Even so the proposals and the model syllabus worked out to reflect the new perspective of Kenya, East Africa, Africa, Third World and the rest of the world, were not readily accepted by the Ministry of Education. They became the subject of a continuing debate and struggle in the educational corridors of power. The proposals were strengthened and argued about in yet other follow-up conferences and in 1981 were still a matter of controversy. In 1982 a syllabus like that of the Literature Department was labelled by some political elements as Marxist. Kenya-centrism or Afrocentrism was now equated with Marxism.

I am not sure if today the proposals have been accepted or not. I think some elements, like the oral literature components, have been introduced in the school literature curriculum. But I expect the controversy continues. For the quest for relevance and the entire literature debate was not really about the admissibility of this or that text, this or that author, though it often expressed itself as such. It was really about the direction, the teaching of literature, as well as of history, politics, and all the other arts and social sciences, ought to take in Africa today. The debate, in other words, was about the inherited colonial education system and the consciousness it necessarily inculcated in the African mind. What directions should an education system take in an Africa wishing to break with neo-colonialism? What should be the philosophy guiding it? How does it want the 'New Africans' to view themselves and their universe? From what base: Afrocentric or Eurocentric? What then are the materials they should be exposed to: and in what order and perspective? Who should be interpreting that material to them: an African or non-African? If African, what kind of African? One who has internalized the colonial world outlook or one attempting to break free from the inherited slave consciousness? And what were the implications of such an education system for the political and economic set up or status quo? In a neo-colonialist context, would such an education system be possible? Would it not in fact come into conflict with political and economic neo-colonialism?

Whether recommendations in the quest for relevance are successful or not ultimately depends on the entire government policy towards culture, education and language, and on where and how it stands in the anti-imperialist process in Africa today.

Whatever the destiny of the 1974 proposals on literature in schools, the values, assumptions and the attitudes underlying the entire 'Nairobi Literature Debate' are today at the heart of the contending social forces in Kenya, in Africa and in the third world and they all boil down to the question of relevance, in philosophical class and national terms.

VI

At the level of the national base for relevance, two conflicting lines have emerged in Kenyan intellectual circles and particularly in the interpretation of history, politics and economic development.

One line identifies with the imperialist heritage, colonial and neo-colonial, and it sees in imperialism the motive force of Kenya's development. The more rapidly Kenya loses her identity in the West and leaves her fate in imperialist interests, the faster will be her development and her movement to the modernity of the twentieth century. This line is particularly clear in the interpretation of history where a corpus of state intellectuals has emerged who now openly write manuals in praise of colonialism. These state intellectuals scoff at the heroic and patriotic struggles of Kenyan people of all the nationalities to free Kenya from the stranglehold of imperialistic capitalism. For them the tradition of collaboration with British imperialism is what brought about independence and not the resistance tradition of Waiyaki, Koitalel, Me Katilili, Markan Singh and Gama Pinto, a tradition carried to new heights by Dedan Kimathi and the Kenya Land and Freedom Army (Mau Mau). For these state intellectuals imperialist Europe is the beginning of Kenya's history and progress. Imperialism created Kenya. Therefore, for these intellectuals, the neo-colonial state is the model instrument for Africa's rapid development.

The other line identifies with the tradition of resistance in all the nationalities. It sees in the activities and actions of ordinary men and women of Kenya, the basis of Kenya's history and progress. The line, best exemplified by the Kenyan intellectuals now in jails, detention camps or in exile – these are clearly *not* state functionaries – insists that Kenya and the needs of Kenya come first. For them, the national perspective in economy (even capitalism if the national capital and enterprise were dominant), politics and culture is of paramount importance. To get the correct national perspective, democracy – where a whole range of opinions, views and voices ran freely be raised – is an absolute minimum. For them the starting point is a democratic Kenya – the Kenya of peasants and workers of all the nationalities with their heritage of languages, cultures, glorious histories of struggle, vast natural and human resources. From this starting point they can radiate outwards to link with the heritage and struggles of other peoples in Africa, the third world peoples, Europe and the Americas; with the struggles of the people the world over, the vast democratic and socialistic forces daily inflicting mortal blows to imperialist capitalism. A study of African literature, culture and history, starting from a national base, would therefore be linked with progressive and democratic trends in world literature, culture and history. For them the quest for relevance is not a call for isolationism but a recognition that national liberation is the basis of an internationalism of all the democratic and social struggles for human equality, justice, peace and progress. For them, the neo-colonial state is the negation of Africa's progress and development. The defeat of imperialism and neo-colonialism and hence the liberation of natural and human resources and the entire productive forces of the nation, would be the beginning of Africa's real progress and development. The national, viewed from the needs and activities of the majority – peasant and workers – is the necessary base for a take-off into the world of the twentieth and twenty-first centuries, the international democratic and socialist community of tomorrow.

The Nairobi Literature Debate and the enormous reactions it generated *for* and *against* reflected the fierce struggle of the two lines in Kenya today. In answering the question – are the sources of our inspiration foreign or national? – the proposed changes implied an unequivocal rejection of the imperialist and foreign and an affirmation of the democratic and national. For the first time since Independence

in 1963, the defenders of imperialist and neo-colonial culture were put
on the defensive.

VII

While the Nairobi Literature Debate has clearly been able to isolate the
national democratic basis of relevance, it has not always been as
successful in isolating the philosophic and class bases of relevance
– although they are implied.

The philosophic and the class bases of relevance are even more
crucial when it comes to the area of critical approaches and
interpretations. For the critic, whether teacher, lecturer, interpreter or
analyst, is a product of a class society. Each child by birth, family or
parents' occupation is brought up in a given class. By education
children are brought up in the culture, values and world outlook of the
dominant class which may or may not be the same as the class of their
birth and family. By choice they may opt for one or the other side in
the class struggles of their day. Therefore their interpretation of
literature and culture and history will be influenced by their
philosophical standpoint, or intellectual base, and their conscious or
unconscious class sympathies.

First the philosophical base. Is a person's standpoint that of idealist
or materialist? Is their mode of thinking and reasoning dialectical or
metaphysical? Does the critic see values, ideas and the spiritual as
superior to material reality? Does the critic see reality as static for all
time or reality as changing all the time? Does the critic see things,
processes, phenomena as linked or as separate mutually exclusive
entities? Since literature, like religion and other areas of culture, is a
reflection of the world of nature and human community, the outlook
of a critic in real life will profoundly affect their interpretation of the
reflected reality.

This is even more true of class sympathies and identification.

A critic who in real life is suspicious of people fighting for liberation
will suspect characters who, though only in a novel, are fighting for
liberation. A critic who in real life is impatient with all the talk about
classes, class struggle, resistance to imperialism, racism and struggles
against racism, of reactionary versus revolutionary violence, will be
equally impatient when he or she finds the same themes dominant in a
work of art. In criticism, as in creative writing, there is an ideological

struggle. A critic's world outlook, his or her class sympathies and values will affect evaluations of Chinua Achebe, Sembene Ousmane, Brecht, Balzac, Shakespeare, Lu Hsun, Garcia Marquez or Alex La Guma.

The quest for relevance calls for more than choice of material. The attitude to the material is also important. Of course, over this, there can never be any legislation. But it is crucial to be alert to the class ideological assumptions behind choices, utterances and evaluations. The choice of what is relevant and the evaluation of a quality is conditioned by the national, class and philosophical base. These factors underlay the controversy attending the whole quest for relevance in the teaching of literature in Kenyan schools and universities.

VIII

For the Nairobi Literature Debate and the quest for relevance were basically challenges as to where people stand in the big social issues of the world today. In the era of imperialism where do we really stand? In a society built on a structure of inequality, where do we stand? Can we remain neutral, cocooned in our libraries and scholarly disciplines, muttering to ourselves: I am only a surgeon; I am a scientist; I am an economist; or I am simply a critic, a teacher, a lecturer? As Brecht says in a poem addressed to the students of the 'Workers' and Peasants' Faculty:

Your science will be valueless, you'll find
And learning will be sterile, if inviting
Unless you pledge your intellect to fighting
Against all enemies of mankind.[17]

Or his poem addressed to Danish working-class actors:

And that is where you
The workers' actors, as you learn and teach
Can play your part creatively in all the struggles
Of men of your time, thereby
Helping, with your seriousness of study and the cheerfulness of knowledge
To turn the struggles into common experience and
Justice into a passion.[18]

When one day the simple men and women of all our countries will, as foreseen in the poem addressed to apolitical intellectuals by the late Guatemalan poet Otto René Castillo, rise and ask us what we did when our nations dried out slowly, 'like a sweet fire, small and alone,' yes when they will ask us –

What did you do when the poor
Suffered, when tenderness
and life
burned out in them?[19]

– we, who teach literature, history, the arts, culture, religions, should be able to answer proudly, like the Brechtian intellectual, we helped turn the struggles into the spheres of common knowledge and, above all, justice into a passion.

IX

The Nairobi Literature Debate is a continuing debate. It is there in East, West, South and North Africa. It is there in the Caribbean. It is there in Asia and Latin America. The relevance of literature. The relevance of art. The relevance of culture. What literature, what art, what culture, what values? For whom, for what? The debate, even for Kenyans, has not for instance settled the issue of multi-national languages in the same country. English is still the linguistic medium of the debate; and of the temporary solutions of the 1968–9 and 1974 conferences. The language question cannot be solved outside the larger arena of economics and politics, or outside the answer to the question of what society we want.

But the search for new directions in language, literature, theatre, poetry, fiction and scholarly studies in Africa is part and parcel of the overall struggles of African people against imperialism in its neo-colonial stage. It is part of that struggle for that world in which my health is not dependent on another's leprosy; my cleanliness not on another's maggot-ridden body; and my humanity not on the buried humanity of others.

A hundred and fifty years ago, that is forty years before the Berlin Conference, a German visionary saw how money taken from the worker and the poor had come to dominate human relations:

It transforms fidelity into infidelity, love into hate, hate into love, virtue into vice, vice into virtue, servant into master, idiocy into intelligence, and intelligence into idiocy ... He who can buy bravery is brave though he be a coward.[20]

He foresaw a new world based on a relationship, not of stolen property, but of human qualities calling forth even more human qualities in all of us:

> Assume man to be man and his relationship to be a human one: then you can exchange love for only love, trust for trust, etc. If you want to enjoy art, you must be an artistically cultivated person; if you want to exercise influence over other people, you must be a person with a stimulating and encouraging effect on other people. Every one of your relations to man and to nature must be a *specific expression*, corresponding to the object of your will, of your *real individual* life. If you love without evoking love in return – that is, if your loving as loving does not produce reciprocal love; if through a *living expression* of yourself as a loving person you do not make yourself a *beloved one*, then your love is impotent – a misfortune.[21]

That was not a German Pope in the Vatican but Karl Marx in the British Museum library. And it was he who threw another challenge to all scholars, all philosophers, all the men and women of letters, all those who in their different disciplines are trying to explain the world. Hitherto, he wrote:

> The philosophers have only *interpreted* the
> the world in various ways; the point,
> however is to *change* it.[22]

Change it? This sentiment is in keeping with the vision of all 'The Wretched of the Earth' in Africa, Asia and Latin America who are struggling for a new economic, political and cultural order free from imperialism in its colonial or in its more subtle but more vicious neo-colonial form. It is the sentiment of all the democratic and socialistic forces for change in the world today, forces once addressed by Brecht in the poem, 'Speech to Danish Working Class Actors on the Art of Observation':

> Today everywhere, from the hundred-storeyed cities
> Over the seas, cross-ploughed by teeming liners
> To the loneliest villages, the word has spread
> That mankind's fate is man alone. Therefore

We now ask you, the actors
Of our time – a time of overthrow and of boundless mastery
Of all nature, even men's own – at last
To change yourselves and show us mankind's world
As it really is: made by men and open to alteration.[23]

This is what this book on the politics of language in African literature has really been about: national, democratic and human liberation. The call for the rediscovery and the resumption of our language is a call for a regenerative reconnection with the millions of revolutionary tongues in Africa and the world over demanding liberation. It is a call for the rediscovery of the real language of humankind: the language of struggle. It is the universal language underlying all speech and words of our history. Struggle. Struggle makes history. Struggle makes us. In struggle is our history, our language and our being. That struggle begins wherever we are; in whatever we do: then we become part of those millions whom Martin Carter once saw sleeping not to dream but dreaming to change the world.

Notes

1 Ngũgĩ wa Thiong'o *Homecoming*, London 1969, p. 145.
2 ibid., p. 146.
3 ibid., p. 146.
4 ibid., p. 150.
5 ibid., p. 148.
6 The debate and the conferences that followed have also been the subject of scholarly dissertations – see for instance, Anne Walmsley *Literature in Kenyan Education – Problems and Choices in Author as Producer Strategy*, M.A. dissertation, Sussex Unversity.
7 Recommendations of the Working Committee, p. 7.
8 ibid., p. 8.
9 ibid., p. 8.
10 ibid., p. 59.
11 ibid., pp. 61–2.
12 ibid., pp. 70–1.
13 ibid., p. 21.
14 ibid., p. 7.
15 ibid., pp. 7–8.
16 ibid., pp. 19–20.
17 Brecht *Collected Poems*, Methuen Edition, p. 450. 'To the Students of Workers' and Peasants Faculty' ll. 5–8.
18 ibid., p. 238. 'Speech to Danish Working-Class Actors on the Art of Observation', ll. 160–6.
19 The whole poem is in, Robert Márquez, ed. *Latin American Revolutionary Poetry*, New York and London 1974.
20 Karl Marx, 1844 *Economic and Philosophic Manuscript*.

21   ibid.
22   Karl Marx *Theses on Feuerbach* No. XI.
23   Brecht *Collected Poems*, Methuen Edition, p. 234, ll. 35–43.

Index

Index

Kane, Cheikh Hamidou, *The Ambiguous Adventure*, 9
KANU, 44
Kariūki na Mūthoni, 71
Kenya, 21, 92; education in, 11–13; government destruction of Kamīrīīthu, 59, 61; and government repression, 61–2; Independence (1963), 34, 38, 44; land question, 44; Mau Mau, 24, 34, 38, 39, 44, 45, 55, 102; and national languages, 28–9; racial violence (1976), 40; state of emergency (1952), 11, 44; US military bases in, 79–80
Kenya African Preliminary Examination, 12
Kenya Cultural Centre, 40
Kenya Festac 77 Drama Group, 39, 40
Kenya Institute of Education, 96
Kenya Land and Freedom Army *see* Mau Mau
Kenya National Theatre, 38, 39, 59; revolt against British domination of, 39–40, 41
Kenya National Union of Teachers (KNUT), 96
Kenyatta, Jomo, 61, 80, 86n; *Facing Mount Kenya*, 37
Kenyatta Foundation, Jomo, 96
Kenyatta University College, xii, 73, 96
Kettle, Arnold, 90
Kezilahabi, Euphrase, 24
Kiambu Music Festival (1954), 39
Kibwana, 39
Kimathi, Dedan, 102
Kimbundu, 23, 29
Kim Chi Ha, 8; *Five Bandits*, 81; *Groundless Rumours*, 81
Kīnyanjui, Kabirū, xii, 35
Kipling, Rudyard, 93
Kisumu, 38
Kiswahili, xi, 6, 12, 23, 29, 39, 41, 72; translation of *Caitaani Mūtharabainī* into, 84
Kitale, 38
Koitalel, 102
Krio, 23
Kuria, Henry, *Nakupenda Lakini*, 39
Kurutu, B. M., *Atakiwa na Polisi*, 39

La Guma, Alex, 105
Lakkenjin, 29
Lamming, George, 76, 95; *In the Castle of My Skin*, 76
land tenure, 44–5, 58
language: as communication, 13–14, 15–17; conflicting phonetic systems of African, 67; as culture, 14–16; as image-forming agent, 15; imposition of colonial language, 16–20; influence of peasantry and working-class on, 68; magical power of, 11; politics of, 87; of real life, 13, 31n; spoken, 13–14, 17; universality of, 15; written, 14, 17, 66–7
Leavis, F. R., 90
Lenin, V. I., 8; *Imperialism, The Highest Stage of Capitalism*, 63, 64
Lingala, 23, 29
literacy, 67; adult, 35, 64

literature, the language of African, 4–33; and Afro-American and Caribbean literature, 97–9; Afro-European, 26–7, 70, 71, 75–6, 77, 87; conference on 'Teaching of African Literature in Kenyan Schools' (1974), 96–102; English and European, 90–4; and English language, 5–13, 19–20, 22, 25, 29, 70–1, 72; epic poetic narratives, 65, 69; Faust theme, 80–1; 'the great Nairobi debate' on (1968), 89–90, 94–6; the novel, 63, 64–5, 68–86; oral, 12, 15, 17, 69, 77–8, 81, 83, 87, 94–5; poetry, 87; and praise poems, 78; the quest for relevance in, 87–8, 102–8; racist, 18, 31–2n, 92, 93
literature bureaus, 67
Liyong, Taban Lo, 94–5
Lonhro multinational, 35
Lu Hsun, 8, 105
Luhya, 23, 29
Luo, 23, 29

Maasai, 29, 84
Maanguuū school, 11
Mang'u school, 39
McKay, Claude, 98
Makerere Students Drama Society, 42
Makerere University College, Uganda, 12, 24, 70, 72, 91, 96; 'A Conference of African Writers of English Expression' (1962), 5–7, 20, 22
Malawi, 19; University, 96
Mann, Thomas, 98; *Dr Faustus*, 80
Markan Singh, 102
Marlowe, Christopher, *Faustus*, 80
Marquez, Garcia, 95, 105
Marx, Karl, 8, 13, 31n, 54, 107
Mau Mau (Kenya Land and Freedom Army), 24, 34, 38, 39, 44, 45, 55, 102
Mazrui, Ali A., 30n
Mboya, P., 24
Me Katilili, 102
Menengai Social Hall, Nakuru, 39
messenger class, development of, 63, 67
Mūkarīre ya Aagīkūyū, 71
Mijikenda, 29
Milton, John, 90, 91
mime, 53–4, 58
missionaries, European, 11, 26, 38, 66–7, 69, 71
Mlapa III of Togo, king, 79
Mobuto, Joseph, President of Zaire, 79, 80
Moi, President of Kenya, 61, 79–80, 86n
Monsarrat, Nicholas, 18, 92
Moohero Ma Tene, 71
Moorhouse, Geoffrey, 30–1n
Mphahlele, Ezekiel, 7, 30n
Mūgo, Professor Mīcere, xi, 39; *The Trial of Dedan Kīmathi*, 39, 43; 'Written Literature and Black Images', 18
multinationals, 2, 35, 44, 55, 70
Mulwa, David, 39
Mūmbi wa Maina, 39, 40

112

113

Index

114